S0-AQM-909

Beyond
Eurocentrism and Multiculturalism:
Volume II

Prophetic Reflections: Notes on Race and Power in America

Cornel West

Common Courage Press · Monroe, Maine

copyright © 1993 by Cornel West
All rights reserved.
Cover design by Norma Whitman
Manufactured in the United States
ISBN 1-56751-006-x, paper
ISBN 1-56751-007-8, cloth
Common Courage Press
P.O. Box 702
Monroe, ME 04951
207-525-0900 fax: 207-525-3068

Library of Congress Cataloging in Publication Data
West, Cornel.
Beyond eurocentrism and multiculturalism / Cornel
West.
P. cm.
Contents: v.1. Prophetic thought in postmodern times
-- v. 2. Prophetic reflections
ISBN 1-56751-005-1 (v. 1.) -- ISBN 1-56751-004-3 (pbk. :
v. 1.) -- ISBN 1-56751-00708 (v. 2). -- ISBN 1-56751-006-X
(pbk. : v. 2)
1. United States--Race relations. 2. Pluralism (Social
sciences)--United States. I. Title.
E185.615.W425 1993
305.8'00973--dc20   92-41610

Second Printing

The "Harlem Address" was given in 1990 at the Studio Museum.

"Charlie Parker Didn't Give a Damn" appeared in *New Perspectives Quarterly,* vol 8, no. 3, Summer 1991.

"Critical Reflections on Art" appeared in *Artforum* in November 1989.

"Black Music and Youth" appeared in the *New York Times* in October 1992.

The "Introduction to Say Amen, Brother!" appeared in *Say Amen, Brother!* William Pipes, Wayne State University Press, New York, 1992.

"Postmodern Culture" appeared in *Columbia History of the American Novel*, 1991.

"On the Influence of Lukács" was given in March 1992.

"The Political Intellectual" appeared in *Universal Abandon?: The Politics of Postmodernism*, Andrew Ross, ed., University of Minnesota Press, 1988.

A World of Ideas interview was given in 1990.

"On Black Radicalism" appeared in *Monthly Review*, September 1988.

"Rethinking Marxism" appeared in *Monthly Review*, February 1987.

"Prophetic Theology" appeared in *The Kairos Covenant: Standing with South African Christians*, Willis Logan, ed., Friendship Press, Meyer Stone Books, New York, 1988.

"We Socialists" appeared in *Crossroads*, July/August 1991.

*To my loving and humble
pastor
Rev. Willie P. Cooke
of Shiloh Baptist Church
Sacramento, California
who exemplifies so much of the best
of Christian faith and black struggle.*

Contents

Part III
Toward Prophetic Action

Foreword

There is one trophy among many that grace the bookshelves in our family room. This one was presented to an eleven year old seventh grader in 1964 for being the most inspirational member of the football team at Will C. Wood Jr. High School in Sacramento, California. Coach Jeffries had never given such a trophy before, but that year he felt it expedient because this bright, accelerated student had exuded such encouragement, was so positive, so upbeat that the morale of the team had been greatly enhanced as a result of his efforts and disposition. Little did we know that this gesture was the beginning of a lifetime of inspiration which would be sown into so many lives with whom this young man interacted.

High standards he set for himself academically, athletically, socially and spiritually. He always looked for the best of what others offered, shunning and downplaying the worst.

With members of his own family, his siblings, he focused on their best qualities and tried to strengthen the weaker traits. His sisters, Cynthia and Cheryl, two and six years his junior, respectively, always looked up to him with love and admiration. They begged their parents not to let him see their report cards for fear of disappointing him with any C's they may have received. Mind you, disappointment, not anger, for they knew his love and positivity was above that level.

His older brother, Clifton, three years his senior, always thought of him as a peer. His insatiable thirst to know as much as Clifton and to do what Clifton did was a given which Clifton accepted with admiration. Clifton was so secure in who he was that he was never intimidated by a younger brother who held him in such awe and wanted to be an integral part of his activities. Clifton's friends such as William Carr even accepted him as their equal. Throughout the years these brothers have grown even closer. They have looked over their younger sisters with loving and tender care.

At the tender age of sixteen he had been accepted at Harvard after having served as student body president of both his junior high school (following the steps of older brother) and senior high school (John F. Kennedy High School), first chair violinist in the school orchestra, very active and outspoken president of the Black Student Union, first-place winner in the two mile track event of the All-City Meet, played second base in the Baseball State Championship Game, officer in the California Scholarship Federation. In June 1970 he graduated with honors from high school six days after his 17th birthday. All of these were accomplished while simultaneously serving as an active member of Shiloh Baptist Church and Sacramento chapter of Jack & Jill of America, Inc.

As a member of the church and this civic and cultural organization, he voiced very strong convictions of what a Christian and community lay person ought to be about in eliminating or at least addressing, in some meaningful manner, the social ills of our society. He was very adamant then and has never waned throughout his adulthood in addressing these issues. We recollect when he and his brother, Clifton, were taken to the Memorial Auditorium to hear the late great Dr. Martin Luther King, Jr. He was about 9 or 10 years of age. He sat attentively listening to every word, absorbing each like a sponge. He cried when he told his sisters of what that experience had meant to him.

The person to whom we refer is the author. It is with utmost thankfulness in our hearts that we can unequivocally state that parenting this bright, high-spirited, loving and compassionate child was a challenge as well as a privilege. He has brought great joy and pride to our lives. We are richer for having had such an experience.

Thy father and thy mother shall be glad, and she that bare thee shall rejoice.

—Proverbs 23:25

His parents
Irene & Clifton West

Introduction

We live on the brink of a new wave of social activism in America. The defeat of the Bush administration unleashes new possibilities to enhance the plight of working and poor people in this country. Bill Clinton has shown that he is a clever and adroit politician. His pivotal victory should signify a crucial turn toward revitalizing the public spheres—from public health care, public education, public transportation to public conversation. Yet this turn will yield significant progress only if prophetic and progressive fellow citizens bring power and pressure to bear on the Clinton administration. Our regulative ideals are four-fold—a more egalitarian redistribution of wealth and power that includes the elimination of poverty, a head-on assault against white supremacist ideas and practices which embraces moral accountability of police power in the inner cities, a monumental pushing back of patriarchal and homophobic structures and a cultural renaissance that gives moral meaning and social hope for citizens in a more free, just—and ecologically sound—future.

As I travel across this nation I sense a deep hunger and thirst for a more compassionate country—one in which public service supercedes private opulence, institutional fairness triumphs over individual greed and the common good prevails over group xenophobia.

My aim in these two volumes is to present in clear, succinct and primarily *spoken* language a prophetic vision of what is worth fighting and dying for as this century comes to a close. I accent the *oral* character of these pieces not simply because most of them are uncut speeches and interviews, but also because they are efforts to connect in a more intimate way with fellow citizens in a conversational mode—much like a prophetic black preacher soliciting critical response from an open-minded yet suspicious congregation. The basic end is not to arrive at one correct solution to the myriad of problems, but rather to forge bonds of trust

ix

and to mutually empower one another to face the tragic facts of the past and present and respond to them in a flexible and courageous manner.

I have selected representative presentations out of the 150 lectures I give yearly at community centers, street corners, art museums, churches, synagogues, conferences, high schools, prisons, universities and on radio and TV. They range from talks in Tulsa, Chicago, Los Angeles, London, Paris, Soweto, Pittsburgh, Addis Ababa, Trenton, Burlington, Atlanta, Toronto, to Harlem.

The principle theme that echoes throughout the volumes is how and why we must go beyond eurocentrism and multiculturalism in order to keep alive prophetic thought and action in our time. For me, this means preserving the best of the black freedom struggle—a struggle that is a species of a radical democratic project that empowers and enhances the wretched of the earth. There are other forms of entree to this project in light of one's own history and heritage. Yet for all the freedom fighters, the unexamined life is not worth living and the examined life is a courageous struggle against all forms of ignorance and power that dehumanize people. This struggle is grounded in human love and human wisdom—the two fundamental requisites for the genuine flowering of we featherless, two-legged, linguistically conscious creatures made in the image of God.

I want to thank Janet Corpus and John Hoffmeyer for suggesting the idea of these volumes to the publisher. And I am grateful to the publisher—my friend Greg Bates—for suggesting the idea to me and executing the entire project.

Cornel West
December 1992

Part I
The Cultural Crisis

The Harlem Address

125th Street and Seventh Avenue was sacred space for the black freedom struggle. On that corner, Marcus Garvey, Malcolm X, Charlene Mitchell, Ella Baker, and a host of others gave so much of their time and energy trying to uplift downtrodden, dignified people. It is humbling to stand at the Studio Museum in Harlem when you understand the tradition of those who came before, trying to make the link between black culture and resistance. At the Apollo Theater right down the street, great divas like Sarah Vaughn and Billie Holiday transformed the absurdity of the black condition into a tragedy—still holding the pathetic at bay—so that heroic resistance could go on, even against the odds. The elegance of a Duke Ellington, the genius of a Charlie Parker or Miles Davis. Not to romanticize these brothers and sisters, but if we're talking about black popular culture, we got to name some names.

I must say, however, that we are now in one of the grimmest moments in the history of American culture—with the creeping self-destructive nihilism among the poor and very poor, and the paralyzing self-pessimism among the stable working class, devastated by deindustrialization: the capitalist strategy to restructure the economy, given the decline of American hegemony after 1973. And then there is the self-serving cynicism and self-indulging hedonism of the well-to-do.

Yes, those are the conditions and circumstances under which cultural workers have to operate at this present moment, this moment of national decline, in which there has been an unprecedented redistribution of the wealth of working people to the well-to-do, a gutting of the nation—into public squalor and private opulence. There has been a vicious realignment of the American electorate by appeals to race and gender and the bashing of gays and lesbians—

3

but primarily by the appeal to race—since the economy began to contract in 1973 and 1974. And on the cultural level, there is a distinctive characteristic of our moment, which is the breakdown of the social systems that nurture our children.

It is interesting when I think about film. I have a son 14 years old and he always tells me, "Daddy,"—he calls me Dad, actually—he says, "Dad, these films are really for me, they're not for you." And there is something to that. The marketing of these films for these children who are undergoing deracination and denudement, the rootless children—not just the one out of two black children and two out of five brown children who live in poverty, not just the one out of five children in America who live in poverty. We are talking about the state of their souls; culturally naked, with no existential moorings, these children have no cultural armor to navigate through the terrorss and traumas of life, to look death in the face, to deal with disease and dread and despair. Culture is, in part, convincing people not to kill themselves, curbing the escalation of suicide. At its best, culture convinces people not to kill others. We have not been too successful: from police to the army, to thugs on the street of all colors, they are targeting people of color, women, gays, and lesbians. I call it the gangsterization of America. In high places, and Ice Cube is just a mirror.

This is what happens in moments of cultural decay. This is what happens in moments of cultural breakdown. And to talk about black culture and resistance means to ask, how do we analyze this present moment and discern some of the sources of vision and hope? Because I look at black culture, and I know it is a bit crude, but I look at it from the vantage point of a freedom fighter. We are not going to be here that long, and culture helps get us about, helps provide the structures of meaning and the structures of feeling which can keep alive the best of the tradition I alluded to before.' Cause that's what *they* did. They were artists, they were cultural workers. Yes, they talked about excellence and elegance, but they always knew that they were dealing with the relentless assaults on black beauty, on black capacity, on black moral character, on black intelligence, on black possibility. They were up against it; and so are we. We don't need David Duke to be reminded.

The question becomes, then, as cultural critics and as cultural artists, how do we generate vision and hope? These are vague notions. They can be interpreted in a variety of different ways, but we have to speak directly and clearly about the need for vision and hope. Within vision, I include analysis, because to be oppressed is, in part, to be limited in exposure—which means being kept relatively ignorant by the external forces imposing that ignorance upon you. That is why those who have the courage—I am not talking about self-righteousness, but courage—those who are willing to take a risk to project vision and analysis and exemplary struggle have to look our present situation in the face. We have to bring critique to bear on those cultural workers, whether they are hiphop artists, or filmmakers, or painters, or professors posing as cultural critics, parasitic on the art objects, pushing careers... Looking at it from the vantage point of black freedom, you see.

We have to be very clear about what we mean when we talk about culture and identity. What is its relation to desire and death, or desires for recognition? Recognition by whom? What is the benchmark? What is the point of reference for the standards that we allude to? The desire for association—association with whom, and for what reasons? Longing to belong with what group, for what reasons?

There is the escalating black neonationalism among young people, and their desire for protection. They know about raw racism, and they respond with raw rage. You saw it when Sister Souljah appeared on the Phil Donahue show. It did scare America, but as Josephine Baker said, "the very idea of America makes me shake, it makes me tremble, it gives me nightmares." And it does for these young people, too. It doesn't justify their limited vision, but it does make them shake and tremble. When they see the police, it gives them nightmares. They have reasons.

One of the roles, functions, of the cultural critic is to sustain a moral vision across the board which is critical of any kind of xenophobia *whatsoever*, even when members of the black community come down on you for doing this. You tell them, "I have nothing personal—I will not allow anything to undermine the moral credibility of the black freedom struggle." Nothing. 'Cause it is the only thing that stands between America's future and the David Dukes of the world. It is not the sole thing, but it is going to be in the vanguard, on the cutting edge. If it weren't for black folks, there would be a Nazi governor in Louisiana right now, you see.

But it also means we have to be attuned to the subtlety of the form and style of art objects, and promote artistic freedom, but be willing to bring critique to bear. And that, of course, is an important role for cultural critics. When we talk about resistance, we can't have monovocal readings of our cultural texts and cultural objects. But most importantly, it means that we have to think seriously about what the conditions of possibility are for creating some political momentum in the black community. Art, in capitalist society, remains a bourgeois space. What I mean is that it remains outside of a context of collective and communal action. There is a difference between singing a song in a church on Sunday to empower a group and singing a song in bourgeois space, or paying money to titillate. There is a difference between beautiful art objects and the particular role that art objects play in constituting a community.

That is to understand religion in the etymological sense. Ain't got nothing to do with theology, nothing to do with dogma and doctrine. *Ligare* means "to bind" and *religare* means "to rebind." And one of the roles of art and cultural work, in relation to freedom struggles, is to try to bind people together enough so that they can be organized and mobilized to bring the power and pressure to bear to transform the status quo, given the silent depression, the slow motion depression in which we live. And that binding has to be across sexual orientation, across race—not because it's cute and a luxury and it's nice to be with white folk and brown folk and be colorful so and so. Hell no. But out of necessity and too much death and disease and destruction in the country. That's the bottom line. And that's what we have to communicate in our art and in our criticism in the most subtle ways, in a self-critical way, and in a loving way.

Charlie Parker
Didn't Give a Damn

Interview in *NPQ*, Summer 1991

In the following interview with *NPQ* Senior Editor Marilyn Berlin Snell, Professor West describes a prophetic pragmatic approach to social change between idealism and cynicism and utilizes jazz as a metaphor for the middle road between invisibility and debilitating anger for black America.

NPQ: Will racism always be with us? Is it possible for us to reach Martin Luther King's mountaintop or is the geography of American racism more realistically described by Sisyphus' eternal incline?

Cornel West: As a Christian, Dr. King assumed that the mountaintop was a regulative ideal, a message of hope that could help us overcome at least some of the many obstacles that lay in our path. He never felt the reality would be identical with the sterling rhetoric.

Hatred of those who have been cast as degraded "other" will always be with any human society. Certainly progress has been made. But progress as well as regress, is an integral part of the rhythm of history. However, this view is not in any way identical with the Sisyphean notion of eternally pushing a rock up a hill just to have it roll to the bottom again. It is not an all or nothing matter. It is better described as an incremental movement forward with progress *and* regress as part of that movement.

American history has always been an interplay between tragic thought and romantic impulse, inescapable evils and transformable evils. To side with Sisyphus on the issue of racism would be to concede that our resistance to evil has meant nothing.

Rather than subscribing to King's idealism or Sisyphean pessimism, I would call for a "prophetic pragmatism" that promotes the possibility of human progress *and* the human impossibility of paradise. On this point, however, it is important to note that though King's rhetoric was idealist, the political dimension of his work represents the best of what prophetic pragmatism is all about.

King's all-embracing moral vision facilitated alliances and coalitions across racial, gender, class, and religious lines. His Gandhian method of nonviolent resistance highlighted forms of love, courage, and discipline worthy of a compassionate prophet. And his interpretation of American civil religion extended the tradition of American jeremiads, a tradition of public exhortation that joins social criticisms of America to moral renewal and admonishes the country to be true to its founding ideals of freedom, equality, and democracy. Finally, King accented the anti-racist and anti-imperialist consequences of taking seriously these ideals.

NPQ: How can the US be both racist and the end of the rainbow for Third World immigrants? How can one society be both the most tolerant and multi-ethnic of all societies, yet still be a land of individual and institutional discrimination?

West: America has always been both deeply xenophobic and a land of relative opportunity.

American society is very distinct in that it has a fluid social structure, allowing relative social mobility. Therefore, persons coming from highly impoverished areas, be they Irish peasants from the potato famine, Vietnamese boat people or Mexican poor people, see advantages here that did not exist in the frozen social structures of their homelands.

The US does indeed have an entrepreneurial sector—as distinct from the corporate sector, which dominates—that provides opportunities to create economic space at the middle and lower levels of the economy. And, of course, there is the public educational system which, deteriorating though it may be, is still available to the general population.

This said, when one talks about the "mainstream" or gaining access to the corporate sector or elite status, things are much more frozen. One has to understand the complexity of America—the benefits of its culture and society—without allowing the elite to get off the hook.

Clearly, there has been progress in the case of blacks with regard to civil and social rights. Today, black poor represent about 28 percent of the black population. Approximately 20 percent of America's blacks are in the middle class. The rest are stable working and slightly unstable working. Thirty years ago only 10 percent of blacks were in the middle class. There is relative fluidity.

There are also more blacks at American colleges and universities today than in 1960, though this fact is somewhat misleading. Today, there are approximately 100 black colleges that educate one out of every two African-American students. And these colleges perform an important role in American society because they are accessible to black working people. They credentialize a group that would not ordinarily have access to colleges. But these institutions remain separate from the predominantly white elite institutions in that they cannot provide access—through connections or prestige of credential—to elite corporate institutions in this society.

The Jewish case in this country is also quite revealing: On the one hand they are a people whose very physical survival often depended on education and literacy. They are a highly literate people who have put a tremendous premium on interpretive skills and intellectual endeavor. When anti-Semitic barriers began to fall—at special elite institutions only within the last 20 to 30 years—highly talented Jewish men and later Jewish women began to make astonishing entrée into institutions they had only recently been excluded from.

However, one does not see the logical movement by Jews from elite educational institutions into the highest lev-

els of corporate America. There are still certain anti-Semitic
barriers at the highest corporate levels, even for a group that
has a history not only of suffering oppression and exploitation but of intellectual excellence.

NPQ: In the battle of utopias between communism
and democracy, democracy prevailed. But if the end of the
Cold War, like the end of dreams, marks the beginning of
responsibility, the US is now being faced with demands
for the delivery of democracy's promise: equality, access
to the American dream, justice, freedom. As you comment
in *The American Evasion of Philosophy,* we are witnessing
a kind of postmodern moment—after the decentering of
Europe, the decolonization of Africa and Asia and the
ascendancy of the US as a world military and cultural
power in the post-World War II era.

African Americans have long been asking America to
live up to its utopian rhetoric; women, too. Now, immigrants from the decolonized regions of Asia, Africa and
Latin America are making similar demands. In a way, aren't
we talking about the paradox of victory?

West: First, for those you have just described, the
choice between democracy and communism has always
been a choice between *dystopias.* On one side there is
repression and regimentation, on the other maldistribution of wealth—but also certain liberties and relative
fluidity in educational opportunities. With choices like
these, who wouldn't choose capitalist democracy? That
doesn't mean we can't be critical. It means we have lives
to lead, kids to feed and dreams of being able to exercise
certain freedoms of speech and worship. We will choose a
place where we at least have a chance, even if the odds
are against us.

For instance, if most black Americans had to make a
choice between communist regimes of repression and regimentation and a capitalist democracy that is deeply racist,
they would still choose capitalist democracy. And rightly
so. But their choice is based on a tragic awareness of their

relative options.

Secondly, though American culture has always been hybrid, it is indeed true that the new immigrants have not only deepened and enriched its hybridity, they joined African Americans, women and others in demands for cultural and intellectual diversity—on the campus and in the corporation.

The immigrant influx since the 1960s came in response to the end of the Age of Europe, the emergence of the US as the world power, and the decolonization of the Third World. There was a decentering of Europe and a centering of the US. And the cultural tradition formed in the wake of these events created the first major subcultures of non-WASP intellectuals as well as non-WASP artists. The emergence of bebop jazz artists must also be noted as an outgrowth of this expansion of "culture."

The sixties really constitute a watershed period in contemporary American intellectual life on college campuses and universities. The inclusion of African Americans, Spanish-speaking Americans, Asian Americans, Native Americans, women, and working-class white men in significant numbers in the academy shattered male WASP cultural pretension and homogeneity. An unfortunate by-product of this tremendous transformation, however, was the jettisoning of intellectual seriousness on the part of both defenders and opponents of the status quo. Nonetheless, this kind of inclusion heralded a complex reconfiguration of American intellectual life that we are still trying to sort out.

NPQ: If the end of isolation is not to signal the beginning of cultural Balkanization in the US, how are we to reconcile the "magnet myth" of *E Pluribus Unum* with the reality of racism and exclusion?

West: The contradiction functions on an economic axis. Until we are honest about that fact, we will do little to reconcile the myth and the reality.

Class now plays a crucial role in terms of limiting life chances for black kids and black people. Gender is also a very important factor. So, when we talk about race and racism only, they become almost *deus ex machina* at the explanatory level.

Though the reality of racism and exclusion is undeniable, racism is not the sole problem. Usually, when Americans talk about race, they are not talking about race in any kind of serious, historical manner. Race is one very crucial and undeniable variable in American society but it is inseparable from economic class and gender.

This said, we cannot allow ourselves to swing to the other extreme, toward Shelby Steele and others like him who want to talk about personal responsibility and hard work as if the reality of racism—*linked* to the economy, *linked* to cultural perception, *linked* to stereotypical images—is not real and concrete and palpable in people's lives.

Steele talks about self-help, self-esteem and individual initiative as opposed to group consciousness and group action for blacks. But the Business Roundtable doesn't operate individually. The National Manufacturers Association doesn't operate individually. The Chamber of Commerce doesn't operate individually. These groups have no qualms about creating collectives. They recognize the power of interest-group coalition-building. They are part of a business class whose interests can indeed be threatened by trade unions and other organized groups and they understand that. There is no reason why working people, or black people, or women or anybody else should not be able to balance individual initiative with collective action. They go hand in hand.

Finally, we have to define "Balkanization." If what we mean are distinctive groups, be it ethnically or racially based, then we are describing collectives we have always had in the US. Balkanization becomes counterproductive, indeed thoroughly negative, only when it precludes or forecloses on the possibility of coalition building. Then, Balkanization means that we are frozen into a closed-ranks mentality that only reinforces our feebleness—*especially* when those who are Balkanized are groups without access to the social bases of power.

NPQ: Is there a qualitative difference in racism between blacks and other minorities in the US?

West: Yes, though morally all racisms have the same status. Historically and psychically, racism against people of African descent has been a targeted assault on black intelligence and black beauty, black capacity and black potentiality.

When one thinks of anti-Jewish racism, which has inspired vicious pogroms, and an indescribable Holocaust, one sees that the attack on Jewish intelligence is very different from the attack on African intelligence. Anti-Semitism in Eastern Europe in the 19th century was horrific, but the intelligence of Jews was never in question; the attacks were justified by certain demonized images propagated by various Christian cultures.

This has not been the case for African Americans. We were three-fifths human, we were monkeys, or rapists. Now we are crack addicts or criminals. We have always been put in a position of having to defend against our dehumanization, a circumstance which often prohibits an honest exploration of just who we actually *are.*

Of course, there are exceptions: One of the reasons jazz is so appealing to large numbers of white Americans is precisely because they feel that in this black musical tradition, not just black musicians but black humanity is being asserted by artists who do not look at themselves in relation to whites or engage in self-pity or white put-down.

This type of active, as opposed to reactive, expression is very rare in any aspect of African-American society. One usually sees either the highly assimilated black person who wants to be accepted by whites no matter what, which is symptomatic of self-doubt, insecurity and lack of power. Or, one sees someone like Louis Farrakhan, who can only assert black humanity by putting others down—a sign of moral immaturity. Unfortunately, those two modes of expression have been dominant in middle-class black America. However, one does *not* find this kind of "reactive" behavior in jazz. Charlie Parker didn't give a damn.

Jazz is the middle road between invisibility and anger. It is where self-confident creativity resides. Black music is paradigmatic of how black persons have best dealt with their humanity, their complexity—their good and bad, negative and positive aspects, without being excessively preoccupied with whites. Duke Ellington, Louis Armstrong and Coltrane were just being themselves. And for whites interested in the humanity of the "other," jazz provides them with examples of sheer and rare genius—a purely American form of artistic grace and elegance emanating from its subjugated people, exiled people, degraded people.

NPQ: In the sixties, spirituals provided the inspiration for an entire movement for civil rights. Today, the culture of refusal gets its inspiration, finds its resonance, in rap music: from "We Shall Overcome" to "The Hate that Hate Made." What does this say about today's "activists"?

West: The civil rights movement was church based and the black church was the foundation for its moral, political action. For every King during this period, there were hundreds of local people promoting universal morality and collective action.

Hip-hop culture is not a movement, per se. Further, unlike the days of the civil rights movement, many of today's mediating institutions—the church, the family, the school—are deteriorating in importance, if not in fact.

Hip-hop culture is based in part on the desire to create an artistic expression of rage. It is conceived and conducted by a group of young black Americans rebelling against their marginalization, their invisibility that only became worse during the Reagan and Bush years. They don't have a movement to appeal to for help. Nor do they have institutions or infrastructures with spiritual and moral vision. They are living in a culture void of hope, a culture in which the rapidly decentralizing production of goods and services is making them obsolete.

But they are also an expression of American culture. These artists are protesting, demanding an end to compromise with whites, but they are also becoming successful entrepreneurs. They are making a commodity of their rage and it is selling—and not just to the inner city. Through this music, a white kid in South Dakota is as likely to find an outlet for his sense of alienation and hopelessness as many black kids in Detroit.

Critical Reflections on Art

Knowledge of art is not enough to make one a critic, any more than knowledge of art is enough to make one an artist. The student who turns to art in order to avoid reflecting upon his condition may become a specialist, a scholar, a connoisseur, but not a critic. For the latter exists through curiosity, indignation, and the widest practice of intellectual freedom.

Harold Rosenberg

The days of art criticism's eclectic and accessible generalists—like Clement Greenberg and Harold Rosenberg—are long gone. Certainly this has something to do with the increasing professionalization of the practice of criticism in general, for the funneling of the creative energy of young critics through academic channels has tended to produce specialists with little sense of (or interest in) synthetic perspectives. And needless to say, this academicization is related in complex ways to the commercialization of art, the ubiquitous commodification of culture in our day.

Yet even given the deadening potential of these processes in all fields, art criticism has lagged behind the theoretical moves made in other branches of cultural criticism. In recent years, there simply have not emerged art critics who have commanded serious intellectual attention on a par with their colleagues in the literary arena. The predominance and preeminence of the grand art historians (E.H. Gombrich, for example) in the highbrow humanist mode has cast a long and troublesome shadow. While literary critics, from the beginning of our century, could draw energy from the erudite analysis of T.S. Eliot and Ezra Pound, springboards that freed them (from old historicist encumbrances) to leap boldly into the Modernist literature of their own day, art critics like Roger Fry, Wyndham Lewis, or Herbert Read remained tethered, despite their admirable

19

attempts to engage with the present, to a backward-looking glance. It is no accident that many noteworthy nonacademic art critics—those who wrote for a wider public—not only for "trade" journals—took their inspiration from Eliot.

This problem was exacerbated after World War II, as the center of the art world shifted from Paris to New York—to a country whose Puritan origins and instrumentalist bent ill equipped its intelligentsia to take painting, photography and sculpture seriously. It is not surprising, then, that the first generation of formidable modern art critics in America were recent European immigrants, or the products of immigrant subcultures—like Greenberg and Rosenberg. And these critics looked to European resources—Trotsky, Freud, Rimbaud, Baudelaire, Picasso—to grasp the new developments in postwar American art.

The entrance of art critics into the academy produced a generation crippled by a collective inferiority complex vis-à-vis the scholarly humanist tradition of old-style art historians; art critics who stood by in utter amazement at the self-confidence of post-Eliot literary critics. And since the slow demise of New Criticism, the brief moment of Northrop Frye's myth criticism, and the French invasion of Jacques Derrida and Michel Foucault in literary criticism, art critics have principally played catch-up. Yet seeking to overthrow, or to undermine, the received tenet that the work of art is, at some fundamental level, independent of the social, political, psychological world in which its creator operates (certainly a worthy goal), the basic thrust of contemporary art criticism has been to deaestheticize (or historicize, sociologize, or psychologize) art objects in order to render them worldly. Hence the major battles in aesthetic theory have been those that pit Kantians of various stripes against different kinds of Hegelians, Marxists, or Freudians. These debates have been and can be fascinating and illuminating—but in the end they prove simply parochial and provincial.

This is so because they presuppose contexts and consensuses that no longer exist. The received modern world of differentiated autonomous spheres, a teleology based on Eurocentric notions of history, determining productive forces, and ego-centered subjects—once legitimate assumptions from which to proceed—has now given way to a world characterized by global commodification, post-colonial and New World histories, nationalist, religious, and xenophobic revivals, and hybrid subjects with shattered superegos. Thus we must now proceed as did Kant, Hegel, Marx, and Freud in their day, namely by acknowledging the ways in which the very act of criticism must construct the new contexts and consensuses in which we should operate. As Rosenberg warned in "Criticism and Its Premises,"

> Unless critical discussion achieves the intellectual scale of our revolutionary epoch, it cannot be taken seriously. In practical fact, current writing on art consists largely of opportunistic sponsorship of trivial novelties and of assertions of personal tastes for which support is sought in pedantic references to art history...As a result, art criticism today is looked down upon by other forms of critical thinking as an unintelligible jargon immersed in an insignificant aestheticism.[1]

Young art critics today would, no doubt, contest Rosenberg's claim by trotting out their new historicism and discursive materialism, inspired by Foucault, Clifford Geertz, Julia Kristeva, and others. And one does find in the recent work of art critics obligatory appeals to history, society, culture, and the role of power. Yet I suggest that this new wave of art criticism is itself another form of aestheticism in disguise. This is so not only because the ironic consciousness that informs this decentering, deconstructing, and dismantling of highbrow European art objects and perspectives is the reflection, in part, of an aestheticizing of art history through the cloudy lens of liberal anti-imperialist guilt; but more important, because it refuses to give an account of how the present historical context shapes its own "historicizing" efforts. If most of our art critics offered such an account, it would be quite apparent that they are actually recycling new forms of Eurocentric parochialism and provincialism in the name of a professional avant-gardism—and one far removed from much of the interesting work of contemporary artists themselves.

The fervent post-Modernism debate in art criticism is a good example of how new historicists, textualists, and materialists wax eloquent about power and subordination, yet provide no analyses of their own deployment of power in regard to what their debate excludes or is silent about. Robert Storr rightly notes,

> To be sure, much postmodernist critical inquiry has centered precisely on the issues of "difference" and "otherness." On the purely theoretical plane the exploration of these concepts has produced some important results, but in the absence of any sustained research into what artists of color and others outside the mainstream might be up to, such discussions became rootless instead of radical.[2]

We might add that the rootlessness—that is, the ahistorical character—of the post-Modernism debate dovetails neatly with aestheticist "weightlessness"—namely, the failure to examine who bears the cost of the "absences" present in one's discourses, and in one's exercise of authority and power.

Part of the problem here is simply the rather racially segregated and discriminatory practices of the art world—much more so than the literary world—which make it much riskier for critics to take seriously art outside the white mainstream. Yet the aesthetic historicism of the new wave of art criticism—which refuses to examine the operations of power at the present historical juncture and what role their own ironic stance is playing in this juncture—tends to reduce this kind of demand to mere moral finger-pointing and pleas for inclusion (as does the belletristic stance of "give-us-back-the-good-old-days" critics like Hilton Kramer).

My point here is not to trash the new historicists—they are often insightful and instructive. Rather, my aim is to emphasize that to be a critic is to do more than reinterpret isolated historical moments with dazzling descriptions, or to cull other disciplines for stunning juxtapositions of cultural and artistic practices. To be a critic is to muster the available resources to respond to the crisis of one's own time—in light of one's view of the past.

The challenge is a formidable one. Walking the tightrope between the Scylla of aestheticism and the Charybdis of reductionisms is difficult. And those few critics who pull it off do so when they are summoned by the power of the art objects that engross their curiosity, not when they follow the dictates of even the most subtle methodology. In this sense, evaluation is never an end in itself (to preserve some eternal canon or further a political cause), but rather an integral by-product of a profound understanding of an art object, of how its form and content produce the multiple effects they do, and of the role it plays in shaping and being shaped by the world of ideas, political conflicts, cultural clashes, and the personal turmoils of its author and audience.

The future of art criticism, then, lies in a more thorough turn toward history, with each step in this turn making possible the next. First, we must require of ourselves a more ambitious structural analysis of the present cultural situation (embracing a wholesale inquiry into both the personal and the institutional operations of power within the academy, the mass media, and the museum and gallery networks). Only then can we focus on the specific art object, according creativity its integrity while conceiving of each artwork's distinctive form and style as a response to the cultural present *and* to past artistic styles. And finally, in examining how significant art objects (those that are accorded stature in the articulated canon, and those that are not) offer insights into the human condition in *specific* times and places, but also shape our view of the current cultural crisis, we will hear the silences and see through the blind spots that exist alongside those insights. Art criticism *is* art history, but much intellectual baggage must be shed if we are to have a criticism commensurate with the complexities and challenges of our epoch; if we are to make history as well as to mine it.

Notes

1. Harold Rosenberg, "Criticism and Its Premises," in *Art on the Edge: Creators and Situations,* Chicago: The University of Chicago Press, 1983, p. 140.
2. Robert Storr, quoted in "The Global Issue: A Symposium," *Art in America,* 77 no. 7, July 1989, p. 88.

Black Music and Youth

The American musical heritage rests, in large part, on the artistic genius of black composers and performers. The revolutionary breakthroughs of Louis Armstrong, the monumental orchestrations of Duke Ellington, the unprecedented rhapsodies of Coleman Hawkins, the serene lyricisms of Lester Young and the subversive virtuosity of Charlie Parker constitute some of the fundamental pillars of American musical composition and improvisation. Similarly, the majestic sorrow of Bessie Smith, the existential joy of Mahalia Jackson, the magnetic understatement of Billie Holiday, the magisterial sophistication of Sarah Vaughan and the technical subtlety of Ella Fitzgerald set the contours for much of American vocal performance. This rich tradition of black music is not only an artistic response to the psychic wounds and social scars of a despised people; more importantly, it enacts in dramatic forms the creativity, dignity, grace and elegance of African-Americans without wallowing in self-pity or wading in white put-down. The black musical tradition is unique in this country because it assumes without question the full humanity of Americans of African descent and thereby allows blacks and others to revel in it. Hence, black music's depictions of the human condition may well be—as novelist Russell Banks has aptly put it—"...our only history without lies (try saying that about any other American music.)"

Like all serious art, spirituals, blues and jazz require of their practitioners high levels of discipline and quality. They also make tough demands on their audiences. In this moment of the pervasive commodification of art and the vast commercialization of music, can the best of the black musical tradition, especially the blues and jazz, speak to young black people? Should we expect young black people to support and listen to the best of black music?

25

Before we rush to answer these questions, we should dispel some prevailing myths about who listens to blues and why. The myth about blues listeners is that they are predominantly white and male, in their late teens and mid-forties, well-educated and affluent. According to Chicago's Bruce Iglauer, president of Alligator Records (the major blues-oriented label), this group is not the only distinctive market for blues. The other is black working class women (and many men) in the deep South over 35. For example, the two best-selling blues albums of the past decade are *Strong Persuader* (Polygram) by Robert Cray, and *Downhome Blues* (Malico) by Z.Z. Hill. Robert Cray received hardly any black radio play, while Z.Z. Hill got only black radio play, mostly in the deep South. The largely white audience that buys Robert Cray—much like those who have skyrocketed the new release of the late Robert Johnson's Grammy-winning complete recordings up the pop charts—are either people who came to blues through the rock-and-roll music of Eric Clapton, Led Zeppelin and the Rolling Stones, or young people hungry for a raw and authentic music of passion and transcendence. The Southern black audience that supports Z.Z. Hill listens to black-oriented radio stations (like WSKN in Montgomery, Alabama) which play blues records—especially those of blues artists established in the '50s and '60s. Notice that young black blues artists are not nurtured on black-oriented radio.

The survival of any art rests on transmittal of skills and sensibilities to new practitioners, as well as exposure to appreciative audiences. Today, the networks of apprenticeship for young black blues artists—as best enacted in jazz by the late Art Blakey—are weak, and the scope of exposure and appreciation among young black audiences is quite limited. If these trends continue, blues music will become the exclusive domain of the older classic artists and a few creative older black and white innovators with only the two distinct markets described earlier—and little or no link to young black America.

The situation in jazz is slightly different. Unlike blues, jazz has sustained a network of apprenticeship that has produced a new generation of young artistic giants such as Wynton Marsalis and Marcus Roberts. Yet preserving a tradition of exposure and appreciation of jazz among young black Americans has proven difficult. Quincy Jones's recent Grammy-winning album, *Back on the Block,* is a gallant effort to educate young black people about the rich heritage of black music. But it is no substitute for the failure of the music industry to target young black consumers with jazz. Since markets both reflect and shape consumer preferences, the decisions of those in the music industry—especially in advertising—can make jazz (and blues) more—or less— available and attractive to young black people.

Besides market exposure, there are deeper reasons as to why much of young black America fails to support jazz and blues. First, black consumers, like any other consumers, are not simply manipulated by the market; they also choose those products that relate directly to their lived experience. Blues and jazz lost much of their black audience in the '50s and '60s when they abandoned black public spaces such as black dances, clubs and street corners. Without access to the participatory rituals in public spaces of black everyday life, blues and jazz became marginal to ordinary working black people in urban centers. In their stead, rhythm and blues, soul music, techno-funk and now hip-hop and new jack style have seized the imagination and pocketbook of young black America. This fundamental shift in the musical tastes of black America resulted from two basic Fordist era features of the larger American culture industry: the profit-driven need to increase the production pace and numbers of records, and hence the reinforcing of fashion, fad and novelty and the overload of black popular musical talent (spilling out of churches and clubs) in search of upward social mobility owing to new opportunities created by the lessening of racist barriers in the industry and wider acceptance of black music by white consumers. Since neither blues nor jazz could satisfy this need or saturate this market, they fell by the cultural wayside—or, at least, were pushed to the margins. The ingenious and quick production aims of Berry Gordy's Motown (with great talents like Marvin Gaye, Stevie Wonder, Gladys Knight, Diana Ross and Mary Wells), Kenneth Gamble and Leon Huff's Philly Sounds (Intruders, O'Jays, The Spinners, Teddy Pendergrass) and the two giants of this new moment, James Brown and Aretha Franklin, solidified this fundamental shift in black music. Furthermore, the present post-Fordist in the American culture industry—of even more rapid (and decentralized) production for global markets by transnational corporations of computerized sounds, programmed music, lip-synching and imagistic dance routines—has encouraged even more talented and socially marginalized young blacks to compete for wealth and status in the music industry. It is no surprise that black hits last a shorter time than white hits on the charts: the selective black audience expects more in less time while cognizant of an overload of young black talent. Is not amateur night every Wednesday at the Apollo Theater in Harlem one of the most aesthetically discriminating and democratic moments in American culture? The pop music industry looks more and more like the National Basketball Association: a rapid succession of marketable young black talent in which even a Michael Jordan (or Anita Baker, God forbid) must hustle to last even a decade against the onrush of new talent in an over-saturated market.

Given this situation, how can blues and jazz attract young black people? Is it possible for these arts to become more rooted in the everyday institutions that socialize and acculturate young blacks? Have not the talents of the black popular artists—talented writers and producers like Babyface and L.A. Reid, Jimmy Jam and Terry Lewis, Teddy Riley, Angela Winbush and KRS-One—edged out any blues or jazz contenders? Is there room enough for all of them? Must blues and jazz artists dilute the integrity of their tradition to gain entrée to this mainstream?

These questions have to do with class and aesthetic issues. After the marginalization of blues and jazz in black American culture, these arts became more and more dependent on educated white people fascinated with the musical genius of their African-American fellow citizens. There have always been loyal black constituencies for blues and jazz, but not enough to support the artists themselves. So blues and jazz took up residence in white clubs, often in bohemian sections of large urban centers, far removed from black communities. There is an increase in the coterie of middle-class blacks now turning out at jazz (not blues) clubs, but they remain a small percentage of those in attendance. If blues, and especially jazz, fail to enter on their own terms in the participatory rituals of black public spaces, they will remain almost exclusively the domain of a small group of older white, Asian and to some extent black middle-class consumers. Yet if blues and jazz make their bid for the intensely market-driven mainstream, can the artistic quality of their traditions be maintained? The temptation is either to rationalize entrée (and more prosperity) in the name of "fusion" or to promote a nostalgic traditionalism that preserves a pristine past in a dogmatic manner. Neither option will do. A rich heritage wanes when a great tradition of the dead fails to inspire and instruct artists whose creativity is based, in part, on a sense of the past. Yet these artists thrive best when they are not simply producers of objects of private consumption but also participants in the everyday rituals of public life in the larger culture. The challenge of the jazz artist today is to navigate between the Scylla of aesthetic hermeticism and the Charybdis of market populism. Young black America may hold the key to reaching such a golden mean. But if the powerful forces of commodification and commercialization cannot be used to yield a new generation of young black people cognizant of their musical tradition, then the highest forms in this tradition—the crucial pillars of the American musical heritage—will lose their anchorage in the black America of the future and all Americans will be more culturally impoverished for this loss.

Introduction to
William H. Pipes'
Say Amen, Brother!

William H. Pipes' book is a neglected classic in an overlooked field of American cultural studies. It is ironic that in this moment of intense interest and inquiry in popular culture—past and present—scholars ignore one of the most rich and lively traditions in our midst: black preaching. With rare exceptions like the literary critic Hortense Spillers, the cultural critic Jon Michael Spencer, and the theologian Henry Mitchell, the complex artistic practice of black preaching has failed to attract the kind of subtle analysis it deserves. The availability of William H. Pipes' *Say Amen, Brother!* to a broad public will help correct this situation.

But why this ignorance of such a crucial dimension of black artistic and cultural life? And given the vast interest in black music, how do we account for the paucity of substantive scholarship about black preaching? In what specific ways will Pipes' text help rectify this situation? First, it is important to note that American preaching per se has not received the kind of academic examination it deserves. This is so primarily because such examination carries little weight in an academy that puts a premium on the written rather than the spoken text. There is an even greater ignorance of black sermonic practices, primarily owing to prevailing stereotypes of black religion as mere emotionalism and cathartic release. Yet on sheer aesthetic grounds preachers such as Black Harry and John Jasper in the past or Manuel Scott and Gardner Taylor in our day deserve the kind of attention given to a Ma Rainey and Bessie Smith or Nat King Cole and Dinah Washington. Furthermore, on social and political grounds, black preaching—in its diverse styles and functions—must be understood if we are to grasp how and why many black communities survived or thrived. So the relative ignorance of the complexity of black sermonic practices—on behalf of black and white scholars of American culture—is rooted in a refusal to take seriously the lived experience of black religious persons as church parishioners, as well as a reluctance to discover how many black people have sustained their sanity in this country.

The study and appreciation of black music is far more developed than that of black preaching for three basic reasons. First, black music is the most original art form created in the U.S. Hence its centrality cannot be overlooked in any serious understanding of American culture. Second, black music is more commodifiable than black preaching. It can be marketed more easily outside of a ritual context, transcending personal beliefs and convictions. This holds even for black religious music, spirituals, and gospels, for example, owing to the universality of rhythms, harmonies, and melodies. Third, black preaching is tied to a certain theological content, namely, its message of the Christian gospel. So it tends to ward off easy reception by those who may be uninterested or even offended by its religious substance.

Yet I do believe that black preaching will become more of an object of serious investigation in the future. The turn toward the study of rhetoric in American cultural studies cannot but mean that research will begin to focus on one of the major sources of pubic rhetoric in the past few decades, as exemplified by Adam Clayton Powell, Jr., Martin Luther King, Jr., and Jesse Louis Jackson. This is especially so in a period in which so few public officials can speak with passion, skill, and insight. The ascendancy of rap music in popular music forces critics to tease out the black sermonic sources of rhythmic rhetoric among young rap artists. This definite but distant link between hip-hop culture and black preaching is fertile soil for any scholar of American culture and art. Lastly, the uncovering of past scholarly works about black preaching will contribute immensely to a focus on its form, content, role and function. William H. Pipes' text is one such work—indeed one of the pioneering works of this sort.

Pipes' scholarship is a breakthrough study in three basic ways. First, it situates and locates black preaching within social, political, and cultural contexts in the past and present. His particular focus is on "old-fashioned" black preaching in Macon County, Georgia—"that part of the 'black belt' which has clung most closely to the conditions of the old days" (p. 4). This focus permits not only a detailed study of a select group (7 in this case) of actual *recorded* sermons but also a comparative study of black preaching over time and space. Pipes' intriguing subtitle, *Old-Time Negro Preaching: A Study in American Frustration,* is significant precisely because it views black sermonic practices as integral to black cultural, social, and political quests for empowerment and emancipation. Similar in theme to James Melvin Washington's brilliant, seminal, and pioneering study of black Baptists, entitled *Frustrated Fellowship: The Black Baptist Quest for Social Power* (1986), Pipes' study is concerned with how black preaching did or did not serve as a vehicle for black progress toward "first-class citizenship" (pp. 8, 89, 107, 132, 142, 155, 158-61). Like Leroi Jones' *Blues People,* which is a social history of black music in light of a human quest for freedom, Pipes' *Say Amen, Brother!* is a cultural history in light of an American quest for black democratic citizenship.

Second, Pipes' historical concerns and political convictions do not lead him to put forward reductionist readings of the sermons he examines. Instead, he gives us subtle interpretations of the forms and styles that go far beyond a crude reportage of their contents. His fascinating examination—aided by the works of Stanislavsky, Freud, and James Weldon Johnson—of the structural intonations, rhythmic syntax, metrical units, and bodily (drum-like) motions of black preaching combines a formal analysis within a particular ritual context and socioeconomic situation. I know of no other study of black sermonic practices written at the time Pipes published his text that operates simultaneously on these different levels of inquiry.

Third, Pipes' work is an exemplary critical history of black cultural practices in that he explicitly assesses a usable past for the present black struggle for democratic citizenship. This usable past enables and equips black people to more effectively and efficaciously acquire first-class citizenship. In fact, his immediate concern with black preaching—alongside his scholarly interest—has to do with the profound crisis of black leadership after the Second World War. Since a disproportionate number of black leaders were preachers, members of the most important institution in black civil society, Pipes' study of their homiletics includes a crucial critique of their impact on black progress. This critique is both candid and harsh. He concludes that the forces of secularization in America —the lures of scientific authority, social mobility, and cultural cosmopolitanism—will more than likely decrease the authority and legitimacy of old-time black preachers. Pipes acknowledges the rise of modern black preachers—those, for example, who were influenced by the towering tutelage of Benjamin Mays and Howard Thurman—and sketches the dilemma of highly educated and socially-conscious black clergy leading less educated and more other-worldly oriented parishioners. He does not discount the contributions the black clergy can make, yet he also refuses to overlook the trials and tribulations they must undergo. For Pipes, one of the obstacles of black progress—besides the racist practices of the larger society—is the fact that (in 1951) old-time black preachers comprise the majority of black leaders. He reminds the small black educated class of writers, educators, and ministers not to "delude themselves into thinking that they are the true Negro leaders" (p. 160). Since Pipes' basic concern is "improving the Negro masses" (p. 160) he calls for a more visionary, sophisticated, and connected black leadership.

The most astonishing moment in this erudite and exciting work is Pipes' rejection of black leaders who are either "economically dependent on the goodwill of prejudiced white persons (which eliminates many college presidents and teachers) or who are economically dependent upon the masses of Negroes (which seems to minimize the effectiveness of the leadership of the average Negro minister, who is dependent upon Negroes for his income)" (p. 160). This claim is astonishing not only for its insight but also for its courage: it is written by a former professor and president of a black college with a Ph.D. from the University of Michigan! Pipes is dispelling two major myths rampant in black America then and now: the myth of the autonomy of black colleges and the myth of the freedom of the black church preacher. The latter is more deeply rooted and widely held than the former. Pipes does not dismiss the importance of black colleges. He simply is candid about the degree to which black educators and administrators in black colleges are severely circumscribed by relatively limited and tainted white financial resources. These resources may not always have strings attached, but decisions made by black college presidents are always affected by considerations of when and from where more monies will come. Even the most visionary and progressive presidents, like Dr. Johnetta Cole of Spelman College in our day, must wrestle with this dilemma.

Similarly, Pipes calls into question the notion that black preachers are the freest leaders in black America. He suggests some may be, but most must cater to the parochial prejudices of their parishioners—as in our day, to sexist and homophobic prejudices—that render most preachers captive and thereby prohibit prophetic leaders to emerge. Pipes forces us to wonder whether Martin Luther King, Jr. could have remained pastor of a black church given his bold and defiant stands against American racism, capitalism, and imperialism, or whether his co-pastorate status and presidency of a group of mainly black prophetic preachers (the

Southern Christian Leadership Conference) actually freed him to be a more prophetic leader. Pipes' book leads one to raise these kinds of rarely asked questions.

Yet Pipes' response to the query about where the new leadership principally will come from is vague, a cry of genuine and heartfelt desperation. He writes, "government workers (postal clerks, etc.), housewives, and retired persons seem to offer the best examples of the most effective type of Negro leaders: they are not always economically dependent on the masses of Negroes or upon prejudiced white people and they have some time to devote to the improvement of their people" (pp. 160-61). Pipes' turn toward the public sphere is salutary, yet he wrote before there was a strong black presence in trade unions of public workers and before there were powerful black public officials. His openness to the leadership of black women is prophetic—the development of such a leadership is still very much in process. And his mention of older black people may be prescient given the demographic balance tipped toward elderly citizens in the next decade or so.

In short, Pipes' challenging text raises some of the most basic questions confronting contemporary cultural critics and freedom fighters in this country—questions of form and content in popular culture, religion and secularism in cultural struggle, the crisis of leadership in progressive politics, and the future of social hope for poor and working peoples in our century and beyond. Yet this is what neglected classic works do: open doors that even four decades later we have yet to walk through.

Postmodern Culture

What do we mean by "postmodern culture?" Does this vague phrase refer to crucial features of contemporary life? Or is it a categorical device deployed by critics and artists to further their own projects? Has the term "postmodern" become such a buzz word that it means anything, refers to everything—hence signifies nothing?

These questions exemplify the degree to which the debate about what does or does not constitute "postmodern culture" is not a mere disagreement about the use or misuse of a phrase but rather a raging battle over how we define and conceive of the role of culture in American society (as well as those abroad). More pointedly, it highlights how we interpret the current crisis in our society and best muster resources from the past and present to alleviate this crisis. Any interpretation of this crisis that alludes to "postmodern culture" presupposes some notions of the modern, modernity, modernization, and modernism—when they began, when they peaked, when they declined, when they ended, what was good and bad about them, and why the advent of "postmodern culture" has emerged. And any use of these notions bears directly and indirectly on how one conceives of what is worth preserving and changing in the present. In this regard the way in which one characterizes "postmodern culture" reflects one's anxieties, frustrations, allegiances, and visions as a critic. In short, one's very intellectual vocation is at stake in one's conception of "postmodern culture."

Because of the promiscuous uses of the adjective "postmodern" in conjunction with philosophy, literature, et al.—and the various reductions of "postmodern culture" to a variety of "postmodernisms"—we must be clear as to the level on which our inquiry proceeds. We are not proceeding at the level of the *popular* mind that usually associates "postmodern culture" with a set of styles, forms, and figures—be it the historical eclecticism of building-making as in the decorative and ornamental references to older styles in the architecture of Michael Graves, Robert Venturi, Philip Johnson, and Robert A.M. Stern, the desequentializing music of John Cage, Laurie Anderson, and Philip Glass, the denarrativizing literature of Donald Barthelme, Ishmael Reed, and John Barth, or the defamiliarizing photography of Barbara Kruger and the early Martha Rosler.

Nor are we proceeding at the level of the *academic* mind that often views "postmodern culture" as a product of the recent French occupation of the American intellectual landscape—be it Jean-François Lyotard's claim about the increasing incredulity toward master narratives (for example, Marxism, Enlightenment rationalism, or Whiggish liberalism), Jean Baudrillard's reflections about the saturation of simulacra and simulations in consumer-driven America, or poststructuralists' (Jacques Derrida or Michel Foucault) pronouncements about decentered, fragmented subjects caught in a labyrinthine world of no escape.

The popular and academic minds tend to be fixated on symptomatic emblems of "postmodern culture," yet we must probe deeper if we are to grapple seriously with our present moment—the moment of postmodern culture. On the one hand, the popular mind is right to see that discourses about postmodernism—especially in architecture, literature, and the arts—were initiated in the United States as a kind of revolt against domesticated modernisms of the academy, museum, and galleries during the Cold War period (1945-89). Since European artists and critics tended to link modernisms with transgression and revolt against authority, their critiques of domesticated modernisms were usually put forward in the name of more radical modernisms. On the other hand, the academic mind is right to note that French post-Marxist issues of difference, otherness, alterity, and marginality are central to "postmodern culture." Ironically, the waning of Marxist influence on the Left Bank of Paris, along with transgressive revolts against homogenizing Communist parties and expanding French bureaucracies, seized the imagination of world-weary ex-New Left academics in the United States caught off-guard by feminist, black, brown, red, gay, and lesbian challenges in the name of identity and community. Yet neither the popular nor the academic mind—given the relative lack of a historical sense of both—fully grasp the major determinants of postmodern culture: the unprecedented impact of market forces on everyday life, including the academy and the art world, the displacement of Europe by America in regard to global *cultural* influence (and imitation), and the increase of political polarization in cultural affairs by national, racial, gender, and sexual orientation, especially within the highly bureaucratized world of ideas and opinions.

These determinants of postmodern culture are inseparable, interdependent, yet not identical. If there is a common denominator, it is the inability of a market-driven American civilization—*the* world power after 1945—to constitute a culture appropriate for its new international (and imperial) status given its vast mass culture, its heterogeneous population, and its frustrated (often alienated) cultural elite of the right and left. Hence, contradictions, paradoxes, and ironies abound. The leading Marxist critic, Fredric Jameson, and an exemplary conservative critic, Hilton Kramer, both view the commodification of culture and the commercialization of the arts as major culprits of our moment, while both are suspicious of liberal cultural administrators who promote these market processes in the name of diversity, pluralism, or multiculturalism. On this matter, the left postmodern journal *October* joins the revivified spirit of T.S. Eliot echoed in the right, modernist periodical *The New Criterion*. Similarly, the uncritical patriotism from above—or, more pointedly, the atavistic and jingoistic mutterings of the cultural right—is paralleled by the uncritical tribalism from below of many of the proponents of multiculturalism, even as both accuse the other of their lack of cosmopolitanism or internationalism. And cultural wars of the canon erupt over bureaucratic turf—managerial positions, tenure jobs, and curriculum offerings—alongside an already multicultural mass culture (especially in popular music), with little public opposition to hi-tech military cannons of mass destruction targeted at tens of thousands of Iraqi civilians in the most massive air attack in human history. In this crude sense, postmodern culture is what we get when a unique capitalist civilization—still grappling with a recent memory of cultural inferiority anxieties toward a decimated and divided Europe—with an unwieldy mass culture of hybridity and heterogeneity and a careerist professional class of museum managers and academic professors tries to create consensus and sustain some semblance of a common culture as a new political and military imperium. These efforts—on behalf of the left, right, and middle—are bold in intent yet often pathetic in consequence. They are bold in that they are unashamedly utopian. Conservative Eurocentrists, liberal pluralists, moderate multiculturalists, and radical feminists or leftists all assume that their grand designs for cultural citizenship in American civilization can be implemented in the face of market forces, bureaucratic demands, and political expediencies in American society. Yet, for the most part, this assumption proves to be false. Instead their efforts tend to be pathetic, that is, they frustrate both themselves and their foes by not only reinforcing dissensus but also undermining the very conditions to debate the nature of the dissensus and the points of radical disagreement. This occurs principally owing to the larger *de facto* segregation by political persuasion, race, and subculture in a balkanized society; it is sustained by suspicion of common vocabularies or bridge-building nomenclatures that facilitate such debate. The collapse of a civic culture, once undergirded by left subgroupings (now gone) and liberal enclaves (now in disarray), contributes greatly to this tribal state of cultural affairs. Conservative ideologies promote a patriotic fervor to replace this collapse—as witnessed in William Buckley's recent call for national service or the melodramatic flag-waving to unify the nation. Yet market forces promote the proliferation of differentiated consumers, with distinct identities, desires, and pleasures to be sold and satisfied, especially in peacetime periods.

But what are these mysterious, seemingly omnipotent "market forces"? Are they not a kind of *deus ex machina* in my formulations? Are they not under human control? If so, whose control? My basic claim is that Hilton Kramer and Fredric Jameson are right: commodification of culture and commercialization of the arts are the major factors in postmodern culture. These powerful social processes can be characterized roughly by a complex interplay between profit-driven corporations and pleasure-hungry consumers in cultural affairs. T.S. Eliot rightly noted decades ago that American society is a deritualized one, with deracinated and denuded individuals "distracted from distraction by distraction"—that is, addicted to stimulation, in part, to evade the boredom and horror Baudelaire saw as the distinctive features of modern life. And in a society and culture that evolves more and more around the buying and selling of commodities for stimulatory pleasures—be it bodily, psychic, or intellectual—people find counsel, consolation, and captivity in mobs, be that mob well-fed or ill-fed, well-housed or homeless, well-clad or ill-clad. And such mobs are easily seduced by fashionable ideas, fashionable clothes, or fashionable xenophobias. This Eliotic insight turns Lyotard's conception of postmodern culture on its head. There is not an increasing incredulity toward master narratives. Instead, the fashionable narratives—not just in the United States but around the world—are nationalist ones, usually xenophobic with strong religious, racial, patriarchal, and homophobic overtones. And Eliot's major followers in postmodern culture chime in quite loudly with this chauvinistic chorus. Yet, many multiculturalists who oppose this chorus simply dance a jingoistic jig to a slightly different tune. In this sense, postmodern culture looks more and more like a rehash of old-style American pluralism with fancy French theories that legitimate racial, gender, and sexual orientational entrée into the new marketplace of power, privilege, and pleasure.

But is this entrée so bad? Is it not the American way now played out in new circumstances and new conditions? Does it not democratize and pluralize the academy, museums, and galleries in a desirable manner? This entrée is not simply desirable, it is imperative. The past exclusion of nonwhite and non-male intellectual and artistic talent from validation and recognition is a moral abomination. And it is the American way—at its best—to correct exclusion with inclusion, to democratize the falsely meritocratic, and to pluralize the rigidly monolithic. Yet it is easy to fall prey to two illusions: first, the notion that inclusion guarantees higher quality and the idea that entrée signifies a significant redistribution of cultural benefits. Inclusion indeed yields new perspectives, critical orientations, and questions. It makes possible new dialogues, frameworks, and outworks. Yet only discipline, energy, and talent can produce quality. And market forces mitigate against intellectual and artistic quality—for the reasons put forward by Thomas Carlyle and John Ruskin, Matthew Arnold and W.E.B. Du Bois, William Morris and Virginia Woolf. Second, entrée of new talent is salutary yet it benefits principally those included. Despite the hoopla about group consciousness and role models, *class* structures—across racial and gender lines—are reinforced and legitimated, not broken down or loosened, by inclusion. And this indeed is the American way—to promote and encourage the myth of classlessness, especially among those guilt-ridden about their upward social mobility or ashamed of their class origins. The relative absence of substantive reflections—not just ritualistic gestures—about class in postmodern culture is continuous with silences and blindnesses in the American past.

These silences and blindnesses hide and conceal an undeniable feature of postmodern culture: the pervasive violence (psychic and physical) and fear of it among all sectors of the population. Critics and theorists usually say little of this matter. Yet in the literary works of contemporary masters like Toni Morrison, Russell Banks, Joyce Carol Oates, or Thomas Pynchon, violence of various sorts looms large in a sophisticated and subtle manner. And most of this violence—with the exception of police treatment of African-American males—is citizen against citizen. The hidden injuries of class, intra-racial hostilities, the machismo identity taken out on women, and the intolerance of gay and lesbian orientations generate deep anxieties and frustrations that often take violent forms. These violent acts—random, unpredictable, sometimes quite brutal—make fear and fright daily companions with life in postmodern culture. The marvels of the technological breakthroughs in communications and information stand side by side with the primitive sense of being haunted by anonymous criminals who have yet to strike. In fact, the dominant element in the imagination of dwellers in postmodern culture may well be this ironic sense of being anesthetized by victims of violence, given its frequent occurrence, and of being perennially aware that you may be next. In this way, postmodern culture is continuous with Eliot's modernist wasteland of futility and anarchy and Poe's modern chamber of horrors.

Part II
Interviews on Politics and the Intellectual

Part II

On the Influence of Lukács

Interview by Eva L. Corredor

Q: Thank you very much for accepting to talk to me about Lukács. What I particularly appreciated in your book, *The Ethical Dimensions of Marxist Thought,* was that your approach to and interpretation of Lukács's work seemed to have an urgency and a relevance to your current preoccupations that I had not found in most other academic critics. I felt that Lukács really "spoke" to you and said something vital to you. In the Introduction, which is very interesting and which is also one of your most recent texts, you mentioned that you felt "seduced" by Lukács and the Frankfurt School, and that it actually happened here at Princeton. So I should like to ask you how it happened, how you encountered Lukács, and which books you read.

West: We had a study group here in the early seventies with a number of graduate students in Philosophy, Political Theory and Social Theory. Mainly, people were studying with Sheldon Wolin. I also was close to Richard Rorty at the time, but Sheldon Wolin was the catalyst for a number of us who came together and began to read Lukács, Foucault, Deleuze, Lyotard and a host of others. We read the Frankfurt School as well, Adorno and Horkheimer. We had some real tensions in that group, and a tension primarily between those of us who thought that Hegelian versions of Marxist theory were the most interesting, and then the anti-Hegelians, mainly linked to the Parisian intellectuals, especially Foucault and Derrida, Foucault probably more than Derrida. Derrida I think is much closer to Hegel than Foucault. We had some wonderful knock-em-out, drag-em-out fights. I was always convinced that Lukács's essay on reification was the most powerful text that I had read, that fused philosophical reflection with an analysis of capitalist society, as well as a sense of urgency as to how to change and transform it. So that essay for me remains one of the great essays in contemporary thought, not just in Marxist tradition, not just in Hegelian philosophy.

Q: So it was *History and Class Consciousness* that you read first? Had you read much of his other works, his literary analyses?

West: No, not at all. In fact I began with the 1923 collection, *History and Class Consciousness,* and then worked backwards and read *Soul and Forms* and *The Theory of the Novel,* and so on. It was primarily the philosophical Lukács, because I actually did not become preoccupied with literary criticism until the mid-late 1970s. Early on, it was primarily the history of philosophy. Actually it was Lukács who led me back to Hegel's *Phenomenology of Spirit.* I had read parts of it but I had read it in a very different way. Lukács sent me back. That was partly because Kojève was an interlocutor. We were reading Kojève's lectures on Hegel at that time.

Q: Was that here or in Paris?

West: No, that was here in Princeton. Not in class, just among ourselves.

Q: I am trying to find out how Lukács might have influenced you in your thinking and what you might have in common. I know that you describe yourself as a "prophetic, Christian, pragmatist freedom fighter," and that you are also conservative in some ways.

West: I guess so, like somebody who wants to preserve something. I would make a distinction between somebody who is in a *preservative* mode, who wants to preserve certain elements, and a *conservative,* that has the thicker ideological connotation.

Q: Based on Lukács's biography that was just published and some books I brought back from Hungary on

Lukács's alleged messianism, one could establish a parallel between you and Lukács in the sense that Lukács can be described as a "messianic, Jewish, Marxist, social critic" and also a conservative. There is the parallel with your religious side. You are a prophetic Christian, and he is said to have been very interested in messianism, especially at the beginning of his career. I am wondering whether you feel that you share a prophetic-messianic religious interest or sentiment with him, or is this something that you would rather not discuss.

West: That is a very good and complex question. First, I think, in Lukács's case, here is someone who, of course early on in his career, starting with existential *Angst*, those very early essays, let us say 1910 to 1917, it is Dostoevsky, it is the problems of life, it is the meaning of life, it is the emptiness of life, it is the spiritual sterility in life that he is grappling with, around the Stefan George Circle, an esoteric but fascinating group. There is always in Lukács an attempt to link quest for meaning with quest for freedom. And the quest for freedom is a kind of quest for deliverance, because it has quasi-religious residues in the quest for meaning. The quest for freedom has primarily a social and political character, but the individual dimension of that quest for freedom is also very important for Lukács. I think in Lukács the quest for meaning and the quest for freedom are inseparable, and that describes part of my own quest. I myself am certainly deeply influenced by Kierkegaard, deeply influenced by Dostoevsky, by a host of persons preoccupied with the meaning of life and the absurdity of the human condition. At the same time, I am also preoccupied with the struggle against injustice, institutional and personal forms of evil, and I see that similar to Lukács's quest for freedom. So the quest for meaning in the Kierkegaardian tradition and the quest for freedom that comes out of a Marxist tradition, does establish some parallel between my own pilgrimage and that of Lukács.

Q: In listening to you, I find a difference in your terminology and the one used by Lukács. Lukács, I believe, thought of himself as a social critic, whereas you describe yourself as a freedom fighter.

West: You are actually right, even though the meaning of an intellectual freedom fighter for me, this fusion of intellectual engagement, political transformation and existential struggle, is so tight that my first identity would be primarily that of a freedom fighter who engages in the fight for intellectual, political, social and existential freedom.

Q: You turn to Marxism but you also affirm that Marxism is not a religion. And again, there is a similarity between you and Lukács that I found in your writings which I should like to quote: You speak of your own "leaps of faith" and that you are embracing "the absurdity of the human condition" (ThDEMT xxvii). In Lukács's biography, which I mentioned to you earlier, the author Kadarkay says that Lukács, and in particular the young Lukács, could "arbitrarily leap from doubt into belief and find relief from the torment of doubt by affirming the absurdity of the human condition" (Kadarkay, 103). I think the parallel is quite striking.

West: Very, very interesting. But I tell you one fundamental divergence between my own view and that of Lukács: for me there is always a dialectic of doubt and faith, of skepticism and leap of faith, so that I am much more influenced by Pascal or Montaigne, who is part of a particular tradition of faith but who understands that the doubt is inscribed within that faith. I am thinking of an Introduction by T.S. Eliot to Pascal's *Pensées,* where he talks of how doubt and faith are intertwined, whereas with Lukács, I think, you do get a quest for certainty that would hold doubt at arm's length, and I am quite critical of something like this.

Q: Yes, I will have questions on this a bit later, if I may. In reading you, I felt that you described yourself primarily as a prophetic man, as a theologian. You are a believer, but you do not speak often of metaphysical things. You remain down here. In that sense, you are more a social critic than a prophet.

West: Yes. If I am in any way prophetic, a prophet without metaphysics, what I mean by that is that I am fairly historicist in my own formulations about how we go about understanding the Real and the Truth, and hence I am talking more in terms of tradition and community than I do simply of truths and facts. So you are absolutely right, I have a *very* strong anti-metaphysical bent. And again, it is very different in Lukács. Lukács would talk not only to make some implicit metaphysical claims but rather explicit ontological claims. He is much more with those who do believe that metaphysical grounding ought to be in place for claims...much more than someone like Dewey or Rorty.

Q: Another question I have relates again to both you and Lukács: You say somewhere that we have a "need for a Simmellian moment." Simmel spoke of "sinful" modern times, which Lukács picked up, in particular in his early work, *The Theory of the Novel*. You yourself have written about "Nihilism in Black America: A Danger that Corrodes from Within," (*Dissent,* Spring 1992). You say that "America is in the midst of a mess of social breakdown...cultural decay is pervasive." Cynicism and nihilism today return very often in your accusations of modern times. The question is, whether "modernism" is really sinful, again, since it was "sinful" for Simmel, it was sinful for Lukács in the early century and, listening to you it is sinful again or still a century later. Is modern age really more sinful than the previous ones?

West: No. I do not think so. I think that we have to understand modernism as a very complex, heterogeneous development with a variety of different streams and strains. The kind of attacks on modernism that Lukács puts forward, I would be quite critical of. That would be too narrow, too truncated in its reading. I think there are some insights there, there is no doubt about it, but we certainly cannot replace history with myths and turn away, internally, from the social and political and attempt to create some kind of fetish of art before which one could pay homage as in fact the social and political struggles were held at arm's length. I think that Lukács's insights there are quite useful, but I do believe that modernism as a very complex development is not one that could be usefully described as "sinful." It has the connotation of blindness, but not sinful. We are talking about the crisis of a civilization. We are talking about the challenges of the people of color. We are talking about the inability of the elite to envision a democratic expansion. We are talking about the rise of the Soviet Union and its attempt to find an alternative to what seems to be a Western crisis in the 1920s. This was a very fascinating moment, but a moment at which it is quite understandable that someone wanted to turn away from history as some arena from which betterment could be procured. Now for me, when I talk about nihilism and cynicism or what have you, especially among the working poor and very poor in the United States, I am talking in fact about the various ways in which commodification and reification completely shattered the institutional buffers for an already devalued, despised and oppressed people, and where therefore the levels of destruction and self-destruction escalate among these people. Levels of destruction and self-destruction that call into question any sense of meaning, struggle and any sense of hope for the future, and especially for any oppressed people in the United States of African descent. The only thing we have really had is some sense of meaning and some sense of hope, and once that is gone, then we are in a living hell, in a Dantesque and most profound hell, and that is actually what we have in some parts of our country.

    Q: I should like to come back to this a bit later and

ask you here about the importance you attach to history. You say that "Rorty's historicist turn was like music to my ears." George Steiner was jestingly criticizing Lukács when he said that Lukács had sold his soul, that he had made a "devil's pact with History" because the devil had promised him the truth (...). Again, there is in both you and Lukács this strong belief in the function of history. What do you see today as major historical conditioners? You say that you strongly believe in historical "conditionedness" of the human existence. So what is conditioning us negatively today, and what in particular is conditioning the poor? Is it capitalism, the government, the drug lords, the mafia? What do we have today that causes this nihilistic outlook and desperation?

West: Two points. One is, that I do not believe in History, capital "H." I am much closer here to Antonio Gramsci; I believe in histories with a small "h," and therefore History with a capital "H," associated with questions of certainty, must go. That's what Steiner means, and that is fine. But histories, with a small "h," with all the specific ways in which over time and space human practices and social practices, both structured and unstructured, go in shaping and molding who we are, that is for me the terrain upon which we are talking about, either progress or regress, betterment or disempowerment. Now when we look at the historical conditions of the present, again I would say one major factor is what I call, loosely, commodification. What I mean by that is simply the degree to which market forces now hold sway in every sphere of our society and in a crucial kind of way echoing Lukács's notion of reification. What happens to a society when in fact market forces saturate a society.

Q: So you think that the drug world is in a way reifying the young people today and makes them into a commodity for capitalist exploiters?

West: They become a commodity. It generates gangster mentalities, because of the question of getting over, as they would put it, instead of getting better, and that gangster mentality promotes a war against all. And it is market driven, because it is a matter of buying and selling, in that case drugs or bodies, primarily women's bodies, but it is market driven. Now I do not want to argue that commodification is the sole force at work today. Not at all. We have got political lethargy, in terms of the political electoral system. We have got a competition between nations that impose constraints upon our economy and nation state to create a public sphere in which there is some vitality rather than squalor. And of course, we have this massive, unprecedented redistribution of wealth from the working people to the well-to-do in the last twenty years. The withdrawal of public provisions has to do with the level of impoverishment, material impoverishment of poor people, which is a very crucial element as well in addition to the cultural consumption. There are a number of forces that act as historical conditioners, but one of the highlights I would still call the force of commodification. Again, Lukács influenced me in this as well.

Q: I found very interesting your periodization of history. As you know, Lukács established the periodization of literary genres, for instance in his *Theory of the Novel.*

West: I liked that about Lukács, even though we know that it could be slightly arbitrary, but we need periodization.

Q: You have proposed two of them which I found interesting, what you call "The Age of Europe," from 1492 to 1945, and then "The American Century," from then on.

West: To 1973, yes.

Q: At the same time, I found interesting that, in speaking of the American century, you also attempted to show the influence of Afro-American culture, for instance, on American music and in general on American style. I mentioned this to some of my colleagues who said that they had never looked at it this way. To Europeans this might be more obvious because of the clearly non-European characteristics of American music, dance, etc., particularly in dance, jazz and the blues. But at the same time, and again, you are very critical of this American century and the modern period—I know, you told me earlier, that you are not *more* critical of this century than of previous ones. You also state that the "Age of Europe" had a negative influence on what is happening right now, being maybe at the root of it.

West: It does have an ambiguous legacy. The great contribution is the institutionalizing of the critiques of arbitrary power, of illegitimate forms of authority, which are *democratic* institutions, but, of course, there are significant racial, sexual and class constraints on those democratic practices, and this is very important in this Age of Europe where it had been overlooked. So it is an ambiguous legacy. You got the white supremacy, the vicious male supremacy, you got class exploitation on the one hand, and you have the hammering out, on the ground, of democratic practices on the other, which are basic for the acceptability of social democracy.

Q: You deplore that there is no strong leadership in this world. Isn't it that in order to be a great leader you have to have a dream or vision. If you look back in history, great leaders usually had some vision, good or bad, to offer to the young by which to inspire them. Martin Luther King had a dream. How do you envisage the future? Do you have a dream or vision for the twenty-first century? In your writings, you actually seem to refuse to voice such a dream or Utopia.

West: Oh yes. I know that is true. But I am not really a dreamer. I have strong anti-Utopian elements given my link to the skeptical tradition. What I do have, though, is a deep, deep commitment to moral convictions and that these moral convictions can be linked to amelioration, can be linked to social betterment, but that amelioration and social betterment are regulated more by moral ideas than a social dream, a dream of a new society, and so forth. Of course, much of this has to do with my own peculiar brand of Christianity. In Christianity, you have a strong anti-Utopian element in terms of talking about human history. If any dreaming is going on at all, it has to do with the coming kingdom. This coming kingdom is such a radical disruption with the present that it is difficult to talk about the kingdom within the realm of human history. So it kind of dangles like some sort of a Kantian regulative ideal.

Q: Let us go back to Marx. You speak critically of people who are "trashing Marxist thought," and of contemporary critics who practice "faddish ironic skepticism."

West: Yes, yes, and they tend to be the same people oftentimes.

Q: Wait, wait, one moment please, since I find that you yourself are sometimes a bit critical of people as well—and I am often sharing your criticism, especially in the case of Derrida and Foucault. In speaking of post-Structuralist critics, you say that "they talk about their subtle relations of rhetoric, knowledge, power, yet they remain silent about *concrete* ways by which people are empowered to resist." With regard to the new historicists, you say that they are "preoccupied with thick descriptions"—I love your terms!—"of the relativity of cultural products while thoroughly distrustful of social explanatory accounts of cultural practice" (xxii). Then you also speak of Foucault in relation to power. You say that you can learn from Foucault about power. As I remember reading Foucault, he is usually *critical* of power, he wants to undo it and show how the power of discourse, for instance, has been used to control individuals.

West: He recognizes no escape. His relational conception of power means that we are always inscribed within some matrix of power, and so we can be critical of the various forms that it takes and the manifestations that it has, but he recognizes that we are always already within a certain matrix of power relations. I think he is absolutely right about that.

Q: At the same time, reading you, you do not see power only as a negative, you want to empower, give power. Are you, in that sense, different from Foucault?

West: Yes and no. On the one hand, I want to talk explicitly about empowerment. Foucault would say, of course, he wants gay comrades to be empowered, if I may say so. On the other hand, though, I am like Foucault skeptical of any concentration of power. This is where my democratic sensibility comes in, because I do believe in fact that a concentration of power does tend to corrupt. I do believe that absolute power corrupts absolutely, and hence needs the democratic mechanism for the accountability of power. But the fact that my starting point is among a relatively powerless people, I have got to be able to talk about power in a positive way, not simply in political terms but also in existential terms. We are dealing with African people whose humanity has been radically called into question. Therefore, you have to talk about empowerment in terms of taking one's humanity for granted or affirming one's humanity, or being able to accentuate one's humanity in conditions in which humanity has been so radically called into question.

Q: I should like to ask you about *"engagement."* In reading you, I felt that in some of your views you seem actually closer to Sartre than to Marx. In *The New York Times Magazine* interview that was published a few months ago (September 15, 1992), the interviewer called you a "young hip Black man in an old white Academy." Did this shock you?

West: Yes, one never knows what one's friends would talk about.

Q: I am picking this up because both Lukács and Sartre were criticized for being social critics but also and maybe foremost, intellectuals and privileged people who did not get their hands dirty. Sartre, in particular, in his ivory tower wrote volume after volume about the bourgeois critic Gustave Flaubert while inciting others to engage in revolutionary action. How do *you* show your engagement beyond your teaching here at this beautiful university?

West: Right, right. I think part of it has to do with my being one of the honorary chairpersons of the Democratic Socialists of America, being part of a great legacy, of Norman Thomas and especially Michael Harrington. As honorary chairperson it forces me to be engaged with issues of labor, feminist issues, anti-homophobic issues, anti-racist issues. It is the leading left organization in the country, maybe the only one, and its numbers doubled in the last few years. In addition, of course, there is also my work in black churches, where I am in touch with ordinary black people.

Q: Do you talk about God at that church?

West: Oh, yes, very much so. I preach on Sundays, so I do talk about God, about social issues, and there is a long tradition of prophetic speaking in this church, the linking of the question of freedom with rich spirituality. We talk about faith and hope and service, so that I am nothing but an extension of a very long prophetic tradition. That is another reason why there is a certain concern I have for tradition, why T.S. Eliot and others mean much to me, even though the tradition that he is talking about is very different from the tradition that I am talking about. But the very *concern* with tradition, also in the work of an Edward Shils, for example, means very much to me. I am deeply concerned about the dynamic character of tradition, except that for me the tradition that I am talking about comes from below and sometimes beneath modernity. It is a tradition of struggling and resisting, black peoples' tradition, whereas the tradition they are talking about tends to be from above. But there is still so much to learn about the heroic tradition in a market society...we need more subversive memory. I think subversive memory is one of the most precious heritages that we have.

Q: This kind of thinking and feeling maybe dictates the amazing sentences you compose, of which I should like to quote a few. About Marxism, you say that "one of the major ironies of our time is that Marxist thought becomes even more relevant after the collapse of Communism in the Soviet Union and Eastern Europe than it was before." You do see the relevance of Marxism today? You are convinced that Marxist thought is an "indispensable tradition for freedom fighters" (xiv)?

West: Oh yes. Very much so. And the reason why that is so is that Marx was fundamentally concerned about the interlocking relation between corporate, financial and political elites who had access to a disproportionate amount of resources, power, prestige and status in society. Certainly, that is a starting point for understanding any society that we know of today, especially the United States. Once we lose sight of the very complex relations between those three sets of elites, corporate, financial-banking and political elites, and the reasons why the working people, the working poor and the very poor, find themselves with very little access to resources— once we lose sight of that, which the Marxist tradition, which was not the only but the primary tradition which would analyze this, once we lose sight of this, then we have little or no analytical tools in our freedom fight. That is why I think that Marxism today becomes even more important, and this is especially so now that Eastern Europe is going to undergo a kind of "latin-americanization" in which market forces become even more important. We see that in Latin America, where corporate America circumscribes local capital, and where the state elites go about carving up and digging up those resources among the masses that remain so tragically impoverished. I think we are going to see a certain kind of "latin-americanization" sweeping across Eastern Europe as the corporate elites and transnational corporations hungrily go searching for markets.

Q: You defend Marxism and the relevance of Marxist thought, including "its ethical dimension after the cold war as an indispensable weapon" in this freedom fight. You stress Marxist ethics. Could you explain what you understand by "Marxist ethics"?

West: Sure. First, I want to make a historical point. Marx is fundamentally a product of Romanticism, one of the great, very complex movements in modern Europe in response to the promise and tragedy of the French Revolution, or as Hazlitt put it, the glad dawn of the morning star, the spring time of the world. That sense of hope and expectation of social transformation, which so much of Europe felt, was lost of course after the Reign of Terror. The second wave of Romanticism in which the fundamental values consisted of the many-sided development of individuals, the values of a harmonious personality that was able to flower and flourish in its own unique and singular way...

Q: This is very Lukácsean...

West: Oh yes, and it comes right out of the *Letters on Aesthetic Education* by the great Schiller. Marx was deeply, deeply influenced by this. But secondly, democracy. This is why I spend so much time trying to show that when Marx defines Communism as a struggle for democracy, in the *Communist Manifesto*, what he means is in fact that these ordinary people, workers, ought to have some control over the conditions of their existence, especially the conditions of their workplace. This is a profoundly democratic idea. Once you link the values of flourishing individuality, a profoundly Romantic notion, with the expansion of democratic operations and practices, I argue that you are at the ethical core of the Marxist project. As we know, Marxist-Communists, Marxist-Leninists and so forth have subverted, bastardized, violated, undermined such ethical claims. But when we look at Marx himself as a thinker in nineteenth-century Europe, driven deeply by these ethical values, although never wanting to be viewed as a moralist—he is concerned about being scientific—we know that these ethical values are deeply inscribed within his own project, and then it seems to me that we recognize that those values have much to say to us.

Q: Some people are opposed to the very idea of ethics, saying that ethics establish something that has to be obeyed or followed. People do not want to be told how to behave.

West: We have to make a distinction between ethical dimension and ethics *per se*, because *every* social issue has an ethical dimension. What I mean by this is that there is some value judgment built into every issue, some moral vantage point from which the world is viewed. This is not solely a moral vantage point, but there is a moral dimension to the vantage point from which the world is viewed. Unfortunately, there has been a reluctance and sometimes downright refusal of Marxists to talk about ethics. I think that has been a major problem. They have tended to displace that ethical discourse with a teleological-historical discourse that is completely unconvincing, catechistic and just raw material for managerial elites to come in like Leninists and then command, regiment and repress the masses. So it seems to me that we have to talk about ethical dimension but also be critical of an ethics that is imposed from on high. I do agree with that kind of critique that one ought not simply impose from on high. As radical democrats, we engage in discourse in which we acknowledge the ethical dimension of what we do and try to persuade persons, one, that the values we hold are convincing, and two, that the ways in which we go about conceiving of what these values lead to regarding our politics, how society ought to be organized, are possible.

Q: Are your own ethics compatible with both Christian and Marxist ethics, or do you find incompatibilities with them?

West: If you believe as I do that Marxism is a particular species of second-wave Romanticism, and if you believe that Romanticism is in many ways a naturalization of much of the Christian narrative about the past and present...(sorry, I interrupted you here!)

Q: Are you treating it as a religion?

West: Well, there are religious residues, I would not say it is a religion *per se*, because religion for me does have something to do with God talk or has something to do with ways of life in which the divine and the sacred are accented, whereas with the naturalization of Christianity and the Romantic movement you do get often the elimination of God talk and you do get a displacement of the divine and sacred with the imaginative and the creative. So I would not call it a religion in that sense, but there are religious residues.

Q: Another approach to Marxism that I found very refreshing in your works was your use of "difference" in naming the areas in which Marxism still would have much to do. This is naturally very different from Derrida's "différance," one of the central terms in his deconstructivism. I found your use refreshing because you are coming back to the literal sense of the word in the real world after twenty years of Derridian playing with the letter "a." So, would you say that race, gender, sexual orientation, age—all these possible differences—have assumed the place of the proletariat in Marxist theory? When you look at them, all these people, all these groups, are not the masses, they are rather marginal, they are outside, they are minorities, not the masses.

West: That is true. First of all, we have to disabuse ourselves of the notion that there ever was this proletariat as logos. The proletariat itself is a construct that is shot through all kinds of divisions, cleavages, and heterogeneities and so on, so that there is the sense that there never is any centering in a group or in the masses, even though the modes of production do create the possibility for such centering, but the notion of proletariat as center and the others as marginal we have to be suspicious of. On the other hand, certainly, we talk about gender, race and sexual orientation, which have *always* been there, therefore it upsets me when people are talking about movements among these people as *new* movements. They are *new* relative to a Marxist discourse, a working class movement. But, my God, the struggle against patriarchy predates 1789.

Q: There have been revolutionary women at the time of the French Revolution, like Olympe de Gouge.

West: Exactly. You take for instance David Walker's *Appeal to Colored Citizens of the World,* which is one of the most powerful critiques ever launched of white supremacy, in 1829! The young Marx is eleven years old. So the struggle has been going on, so they are not really new social movements but they are significant social movements. I do think that we have to talk about alliance and coalition because none of these movements in and of themselves or by themselves has the power to deal with the rule of capital, that is the rule of those interlocking elites I was talking about. Oftentimes some versions of these social movements based on race, gender and sexual orientation do not even talk about the role of corporate power which is as limiting and limited as one can imagine.

Q: Are you optimistic enough to believe that this will change eventually?

West: Oh sure, oh sure! Well, it is going to be a long process. I think Raymond Williams's "long revolution" is an apt metaphor. But there are many of us who will go down fighting, trying to ensure that linkages are made, so that we can target the role of these elites not in any vulgar or immoral way but simply acknowledge the degree to which they had this disproportionate amount of power and resources that ought to be shared and distributed within constitutional constraints.

Q: You are very laudatory about sophisticated Marxist theory, you say that it is indispensable, but then you also feel that it is inadequate. It is not complete. It is not enough. Where do you see its shortcomings? What else is necessary? Where do you find or get what is necessary?

West: The Marxist tradition has no serious or subtle conception of culture, and by culture I mean the sphere of desire and pleasure, the various quests for identities, e.g. nationalism. Eric Hobbsbaum's recent book on nationalism is a good example of this, a good example because it shows some of the insights of Marxism on nationalism. We know that nationalism is primarily about elites' carving up territories in order to control markets and control populations. That is true for any kind of bourgeoisie that casts itself on a nationalist mode. We also know about nationalists' desire for association, recognition, and protection, which all has to do with desire, with how you bestow meaning upon yourself, with notions of mortality and notions of monumentality that still have hold on men's imagination. So nationalism must be understood as a psycho-cultural phenomenon as well as an institutional phenomenon among elites. You see Marxism simply does not speak to the levels of psycho-cultural politics. You need Freud…and you need novels, you need the blues and spirituals, a whole host of other insights.

Q: I teach future officers, future leaders, among them there are some minorities, blacks, women. I was wondering what you would tell them. What would you tell them to read?

West: Well, one, they should read a lot of history. They could begin with Paul Kennedy's book on *The Rise and Fall of Great Powers,* so that they would have a sense of where America is now, so that as future leaders they have a sense of the general sweep of the last 75 or 100 years. Secondly, they should read histories that help give an account of how they now have opportunities in places, whereas they had those opportunities denied before, and what the nature of those struggles were that made them gain access to such privileged spaces in American society, how difficult, protracted and how sacrificial those struggles were, and then try to situate themselves in relation to that tradition of struggle. But that is a tough one because, you know, there are always "betwixt and betweens" being at the Naval Academy and that deep conservatism, deep suspicion of any radical critique both for intellectual as well as personal and career reasons. They have to struggle with that. They've got to wrestle with that.

Q: I am teaching a course in French Civilization in which I sometimes speak of contemporary criticism, and I have noticed that in particular my black students are usually very interested in contemporary criticism, even in theories such as Derrida's deconstruction, when I bring in some examples as to how it could be used in social criticism concerning blacks or women in the deconstruction of established discourse. My black students are usually much more interested in this than the average white midshipman to whom it is not of great urgency. I am thinking of one of my students in particular to whom I sometimes talk about such theories and who seems to have questions concerning them.

West: Racism is everywhere these days, sexism is everywhere in society, so they experience themselves as *other*, as you can imagine, in some way even degraded at the Naval Academy or Princeton or any other elite place. These are theories that speak to that condition, I would imagine.

Q: I think it would be wonderful to have you down there but I am sure we cannot afford you, I don't know.

West: No, no. I would love to come. I was thinking of North Carolina. But Maryland is not that far. I am going to be preaching in Annapolis this summer.

Q: Are you! During the summer midshipmen are not going to be there. You should come during the school year.

West: Well, maybe I'll wait until the fall. We'll work

something out.

Q: We have a Black Studies Club at the Academy which you could address. Now, I should like to come back to something which I think is characteristic of the methodology you use in your essays on Marxist ethics. You seem to support very strongly the idea of "radical historicism" and be critical, almost in a purist fashion, of those who do not adhere to it, including Engels. In your analyses of Feuerbach, again, it is interesting to note *what* you single out for your discussion and *how* you define radical historicism. You virtually do away with the Marxist Utopia. You see radical historicism as a process of which you approve, which you love, if I may say so, and which you embrace. This is, in your view, what historicism should be.

West: Yes, this is a very, very significant point. Actually I do the same thing in my essay on Jameson. I think that is just a built-in bias, and in the end it may be unjustified. That is a built-in bias against Utopianism, and yet for so much of any quest for freedom the Utopian dimension is crucial. I want to make a distinction between human hope and a Utopian quest, because human hope for me is always being able to keep going, to sustain struggle, with ideals, but that is very different from a Utopian impulse where you try to project a whole different and better society that could be realized and actualized. I am suspicious of the latter.

Q: You like process, praxis and continuation. I have written down at least ten notions that you reject. Here are a few: rational necessity, universal obligation, philosophical certainty, eternal truth. How can you reconcile this with your prophetic approach?

West: That's right. It is a peculiar, peculiar kind of prophetic, because my conception of the prophetic is not one in which one speaks from on top, which is continuous with the great and grand Jewish and Christian traditions of the prophetic that I know of, in which "Thus says the

Lord," or "Eternal truth speaks from on top." My notion of the prophetic is a democratic one in which, in the midst of the quotidian, the commonplace, in the midst of the messy struggle in which one's hands are dirty, that one is holding on to moral convictions and tries to convince others that they ought to be accepted even though these moral convictions themselves can still be subject to criticism and change in vision and what-have-you.

Q: You are really preaching *hope*, I think.

West: That's it. That's right. But it is a hope that is grounded in a particular messy struggle and it is tarnished by any kind of naive projections of a better future, *so that it is hope on the tight rope* rather than a Utopian projection that looks over and beyond the present and oftentimes loses sight of the present.

Q: In many ways, you are quite Pascalian. The Pascalian wager is there and also Pascal's *"Essayons donc de bien penser."* This is really what you are preaching.

West: Exactly. You hit the nail on the head, in the sense that my Pascalian sensibility is probably my central sensibility.

Q: Again it is a stress on the process, the thinking, the being process. But I think, to come back to Lukács, that you credit Lukács too much for being a process theoretician. For Lukács it is very important that "what there is" today is bad, and he seems to have a definite idea of "what there ought to be." There is in him at least this teleological drive toward what there ought to be. I like your interpretation, because I think you are "updating" Lukács, in this sense you are going beyond his limitations. I have often felt that Lukács's theories were too closed, that he used too many norms, for instance for "realism." You emphasize the importance of process. Is it a dialectic process?

West: Again, for me the dialectic is understood in a heuristic way rather than an ontological way, and what I mean by that is that it is a dialectic that is positive in order to keep the process going rather than a dialectic that is somehow inherent in and implanted within the real. And so I want to keep the process going, and I see dialectic as a very crucial means of doing that both practically and theoretically. And, of course, what we mean by dialectic, and this is what I love about Lukács, is his concern with protracted struggle.

Q: In trying to identify your values, locating them in your texts, I was amazed by some of your statements that seemed almost metaphysical, for instance when you speak of "sacrificial love"...

West: There is nothing metaphysical about it. It is just almost sublime, you know, because the thing about sacrificial love is that it has no metaphysical foundation for it. It is simply a leap that we make in our short lives that gives it so much meaning and infuses it with so much significance. It is a dangling experience. You take a tremendous risk, you become tremendously vulnerable, but there is no metaphysical ground. No security, nothing guaranteed, no surety whatsoever.

Q: There are no truths that you are clinging to. The quest for truth and philosophical certainty are anathema to the kind of radical historicism which you admire. Again, you are maybe Pascalian in the sense that you recognize an end to what humans can do and can understand, and simply subscribe to the process of life and its own limits. You affirm life and have hope and maybe faith in life.

West: Well, in addition to the Pascalian sensibility, I have a deep Chekhovian strain. What is so great about Chekhov? I think he understood this better than others, that we are able to love, care, and serve others—and this is so true of his life and his art—but we are able to do that with there being no deep faith in life or human nature or history or what-have-you. And then it does not mean that we are anti-life, it does not mean that we are cynical toward it, it is simply there, and we do these things because, given our tradition that has shaped us, we do in fact feel that it does give life so much meaning and richness and so forth. Now, as a Christian, I do this against the backdrop of certain narratives, the Gospel, the synoptic Gospel narratives, but again there is no metaphysical underbearing.

Q: In reading such ideas in your text, it made me think of Camus. Camus says that the only thing we can do is give affection, joy, and share in it. I am thinking of *The Plague,* in which the doctor continues to treat his plague-stricken patients in the midst of all hopelessness. This gives his life essence, quality. And it is not metaphysical in Camus either.

West: There are lots of parallels between him and Chekhov. I still think Chekhov had the highest expression of this deep sense of love, and care, and struggle, and service. It is just that for him, it is not against the Christian backdrop as it is for me.

Q: I am coming to the end of my questions. In that article in *The New York Times,* they described you as a great "synthesizer," and I see that in you as well. You bring together contradictions, you are a black star at a white academy, you are a believing Christian in a secular society, you are a progressive socialist in the age of capitalism, a cosmopolitan, public intellectual among academic specialists, a radical traditionalist. Do you see yourself in those descriptions? Do you have a calling to bring together seeming contradictions?

West: It certainly is to build on the best of Lukács, which promotes synthetic and synoptic views and visions of the past and present. In fact, one of the things I said before, one of the things I *love* about Lukács is this synecdochical mode of thinking in which you always try to relate parts to a whole, with notions of totality, even for me heuristically posited, that are very important in that they highlight interrelations and dependencies.

Q: Is the notion of totality important to your thinking?

West: Oh yes. Very important.

Q: How can you reconcile this with your admiration for Deleuze?

West: No, I think Deleuze is wrong about this. I think post-Structuralists are wrong about this. I think they are right to trash certain conceptions of totality that elide and elude difference and diversity, heterogeneity and alterity, and so forth. But I think that they have done away with totalities *per se*. I think we need to posit totalities with all the openness and flexibility that one can muster, but we must posit totalities in order to look at the dynamic relation between parts.

Q: I am coming to my final question. In your present prophetic pragmatism, is there a Lukács, and where is he? What is his future there?

West: Of course, politically, there is no Lukács at all in terms of his links to Stalinism. I actually believed that there was a Luxembourgist moment in the early Lukács that has been overlooked, but the general association of Lukács with Stalinism is in fact quite empirically verifiable and therefore there are no political links for me in this regard. Philosophically and intellectually, there are strong links, because my vantage point from looking at modern society, especially American society, remains the processes of reification and commodification. That is where I begin. So there is always a Lukácsean beginning. Methodologically, I begin with synecdochical ways of looking at the world, the relation of parts to a totality. So again, I believe, that is deeply Lukácsean, even though he has no monopoly on it, because there is the Christian view about relations of parts and whole, and there is the Hegelian one, but I mean Lukács is part of this Hegelian-Marxist sweep in terms of the relationship between the parts and the whole. The Lukácsean moment for me would be on two levels, on the methodological and the philosophical level.

The irony is, here I am, as a black Christian, deeply

indebted to the Marxist tradition, to Pascal, Chekhov, the blues, spirituals, the black church and what-have-you, defending certain distinctive elements in Lukács's project and yet, at the same time, recognizing that Marxist theory and Marxist secular sensibility are both indispensable *and* inadequate, something to build on but also something to bring serious critique to bear on. The same values of individuality and democracy that I see in Marx, in Schiller and the democratic tradition, now also filter through the best of the black church, leads me to this radically secular Budapest-born Marxist, even though I come from "the hood." In this sense, the struggle for human freedom is indivisible.

Q: I am not surprised that you do not stop at Lukács, that you do not take him as an end in itself, nor anyone or anything else for that matter. That would be contrary to your approach to everything. Continuation and process are natural to you and your quest.

Would you like to add a final note to our discussion?

West: No, not really. I think this is one of the best interviews I have had. What you have actually led me to see in myself I rarely get a chance to think about. I am on the run all the time and do not really get a chance to think about, especially, this Pascalian-Chekhov stuff.

Q: Thank you very much. I hope you will come to preach in Annapolis and talk to my students.

On The Future of
the Black Church

Interview by Paul Ruffins

Q: What do you see as the Church's future role in black empowerment?

West: The black church is going to have to change in order to meet new challenges. Its leadership is going to have to become much more sophisticated, critical and self-critical. This is the only way that democratic sensibilities can become more pronounced and pervasive in the black community. Second, it has to become more grounded in intellectual inquiry. We can no longer have leaders who engage simply and primarily in putting forth moral condemnation and ethical rhetoric without any understanding of how power and wealth operate in this society.

Q: How is that going to be different? The black church was thought to be the backbone of the Civil Rights movement.

West: We will now have a two-pronged strategy. We no longer will be involved primarily in protest from the outside. We will have sophisticated clergy who will be able to work from within, such as the Bill Grays (D-PA) and the Walter Fauntroys (D-DC). However, there's still a need for sophisticated protest leaders. Too much of the talent has gone inside the establishment and has gotten caught in the rough-and-ready process of trying to reach some political consensus. It's a tremendous problem reflected in the ways in which that vacuum has now been filled or at least attempted to be filled by the Farrakhans, the early Al Sharpton and others. Today, we don't have protest leaders of the quality of the Malcolm X's and the

Kings who had political skills but also had a broad moral vision.

Q: In one of your papers you communicated a kind of disdain for the manager. Is that fair? Isn't there a role for the black mayor who isn't a protest leader but may just be a good competent manager?

West: I don't disdain management. In the contemporary world in which we live you must have efficiency and good management. The problem is when management and efficiency become the primary values. Management without a prophetic or spiritual vision is hollow, in the same way that the vision without the management seems to be impotent. The question is, how do you bring the two together. Someone like Harold Washington acknowledged the crucial role of good management but also knew that good management in and of itself is never sufficient. There has to be vision, there has to be critique of what one is managing.

Q: Do you find there is a big problem with self-criticism in the church?

West: Oh, very much so. Of course, this is also true of America in general. But in black churches especially, there are certain constraints on the capacity to be critical and self-critical because there is so much invested in "leadership" and the leaders do not see criticism and self-criticism as enhancing their position. What we're talking about, in part, is the empowerment of laity and the empowerment of the small minority of the best black church leaders who are critical and self-critical. These are the men and women we must look to for leadership that is courageous in action and sophisticated in analysis, because criticism is inextricably bound to democratic sentiments and sensibility.

Q: Do you see that people like Malcolm X and Martin Luther King were the results of this type of self-criticism?

West: Yes and no. All prophets, even the great ones like Malcolm and Martin and Fannie Lou Hamer and Ella

Baker are imperfect. Therefore, on one hand, we can highlight their great strengths, but they had negative aspects as well. For example, Malcolm X was never self-critical about the role of Islam in the world, especially its conservative versions, and King was not self-critical enough in terms of gender issues and homophobia.

We need to make self-criticism a perennial process. Malcolm X and King were part of the critical aspects of their time though they were still not critical enough.

Q: They were critics but not self-critics?

West: They were self-critical in a certain sense, but not enough. When King later talked about economic injustice more so than he did early on, and when Malcolm X talked about moral universalism as opposed to his earlier moral particularism, those were signs of growth and development as a result of criticism and self-criticism.

Q: You say that the church must understand wealth. Do you see that the black church will have to play an increasing economic role?

West: Very much so, in two ways. First, it has got to become a better caretaker of the resources that it garners from its congregations. We need a more morally responsible political economy of the church. We must know where the resources are going, how they are helping to empower people, and what the distribution of that wealth is within these institutions, vis-à-vis leadership and laity. The second is the role that the churches are going to play as economic institutions in and of themselves. We're entering a period in which many black communities are in a political, social and economic state of siege. People are searching for black institutions that have some self-sufficiency. The black church has a critical role in helping to create more viable economic infrastructures in our community because we need economic resources for a variety of progressive purposes, from housing for the elderly, to credit unions, to advancing capital for black business.

Q: So you see that the church will have both an

expanded role and an expanded need to deal with that role on a sophisticated basis.

West: I think we ought not have any illusions about this, in that the black church does not have the economic resources to meet the enormous problems of the black community, especially the black poor. However, the black church can do much better than it's doing now in terms of promoting self-help and self-sufficiency. Yet self-help and self-sufficiency are not in and of themselves enough; the black church must be part of a larger political agenda in terms of creating more effective government programs to help the poor.

Q: Recently, there has been a lot of criticism about looking to the government for help. Don't you think the answer is for the black church and middle class to try and provide more services to the black poor ourselves?

West: No. I do not support the notion that black philanthropy or middle class giving will have any kind of serious impact on the black poor. That does not mean that we ought not to give, or do what we can. However, I believe that the most important issues are structural and institutional. I take the traditional view that we must put pressure on the government to put forth programs that can effectively solve the problems because the government has the resources. I feel that the black middle class should render services to the poor through institutions such as the church, not as individuals. Finally, at an economic level, the issues of joblessness, unemployment and underemployment are issues that must be pushed by the black middle class as part of a larger coalition with labor and feminists, gays and lesbians and other organizations.

Q: Why shouldn't we depend more on the black middle class to directly help the black poor?

West: Because no middle class in America, even the most successful, which are the Jewish and Japanese Americans, has been able to support its own poor by means of direct giving. So if the strongest, smallest, ethnic middle classes without a history of slavery or second class citizenship cannot do it, then it's unreasonable to expect that the black middle class that's much more fragile economically, and more anxiety-ridden psychologically, can do it. In fact, it just creates more guilt and anxiety to maintain that we have both the capacity and the responsibility to completely rescue the black poor. We have a responsibility to enhance the conditions of the black poor by means of structures and institutions; black churches, fraternities, etc., but we don't have the capacity to do it. We do have a few upper-middle class individuals who surface and have their own moral responsibilities, but even they can't do it. William Wilson's theory that middle class flight helped create the social disintegration of the underclass is only half of it. He is correct that there is no longer much trans-class linkage between the black middle class and the black poor. However, economically, the black middle class had nothing to do with the history of joblessness and unemployment facing the underclass. That's part of the larger structural and economic problems of black America which the black middle class, who are primarily white collar workers, has no control over.

Q: What do you feel about the criticism that blacks and liberals are wrong to still be looking to the government for help?

West: The attempt to make government responsible to disadvantaged citizens is an idea that will never go away in the modern world. It's inescapable, and corporations adopt the same idea when they feel themselves to be disadvantaged. That's why Chrysler was bailed out. The problem is that over the last twenty years, the programs we've designed haven't been good enough, partly because they were compromises that still allowed for corporate domination of the economy and government, while providing a certain welfare for the poor. Our challenge is to come up with better programs that are more effective. That doesn't mean that the government is a panacea for all ills.

It is true that cultural and moral decay cannot be fundamentally solved by means of government. By decay I mean people who think their lives are meaningless, people who put very little value on their life, persons who find themselves unable to sustain meaningful relationships. Our society is experiencing a lot of disintegration; rising suicides and the reduction of human relations to bodily stimulation. Our culture of consumption says that one finds meaning through possessions. And in the black community there is a particularly acute spiritual crisis of meaning. People look to the church and they find similar materialism and consumerism within religious forms. They look for meaning in political movements and they find hucksterism and charlatanism which is nothing but the egoism that is found in the mainstream of society.

People are looking for places where some value and meaning can be found outside of a market-based conception of life, and this is where a prophetic church, this is where a prophetic political movement can play a role.

Q: How do you see the role of the church in solving these problems? It seems it hasn't been very effective in reaching the people who no longer participate in the church.

West: Without the churches we would be in much worse shape. So we must acknowledge that they are already playing an important, even if not sufficient, role in holding back the meaninglessness and hopelessness that impinges on large numbers of black people.

Q: How do churches' political activities fit into the issue of building meaning?

West: Look at the Jackson campaign. Jackson is a child of the black church who went from being a protest leader to a power broker in the Democratic Party. He leapfrogged over the black political class, over the black elected officials, to play in the big game of presidential politics. Because of his power base in the black church, he has a freedom to say things that other mainstream politicians can't say. He has proven that the black church can produce leaders that speak with passion and power, but are sophisticated enough to engage in coalitional politics, and who are broad-based enough to project visions and programs that cross gender and class lines. At a cultural level the Jackson campaign has helped fill this void, by showing people that it's possible to be a person against the culture of consumption, to find meaning outside of an orgiastic addiction to sexual and other kinds of stimulation.

Q: On a non-political level, many people argue that the solution is a return to traditional conservative morality, with men in charge of families, etc.

West: Those are options of desperation. Nostalgia cannot help us in any meaningful way. There is no turning back the clock of time. This is true for both Christians and non-Christians. The male-dominated family, the traditional forms of giving meaning to life no longer function in an effective way.

Q: But isn't that the problem?

West: Perhaps, but you can never go back. You can only build on the best of the tradition and allow for that tradition to grow and develop in relation to the new. That's what the old folks did.

Q: Can you give us a specific example?

West: A great example would be Benjamin Mays. Mays had been trained in the fundamental black church tradition in the red hills of Georgia. But when he goes to the University of Chicago, he realizes that he has to acknowledge the modern challenge to Christianity, particularly black Christianity. He remains grounded in the black church, but he recognizes that in order to produce new leadership, they have to be grounded in social scientific perspectives and in anti-colonial struggles like Gandhi in India, to see whether such strategies can be applied in the United States, and we can see his impact on the young Martin Luther King who was an undergraduate at

Morehouse.

It's only by looking the new in the face, the future in the face, being open enough to revise and transform the tradition and reject the worst of it, will one be able to build something better upon it. We can never repeat or imitate the Benjamin Mayses, the Martin Luther Kings, the others. We have to do what they did, in our time, which is to be creative; appropriate the best of the old, but also project the new. And for me that means taking seriously the role of black women, rejecting the marginalization of lesbians and gays, and understanding the role of class in our social structure; understanding what Jesse Jackson would call economic violence.

Q: You seem to see a significant role for sexual minorities. Isn't that unusual for a professor of religion?

West: Part of this is that on moral grounds we have to come to grips with the fact that we have a variety of sexual experiences in our community and that we can no longer afford to immorally marginalize people and therefore limit their lives and deprive the community of their talents. This is primarily an affirmation of diversity, and one that black people must understand.

Traditionally black people have labored under the notion that we must have some homogeneity in order to be strong. They confuse homogeneity with unity. These are not the same thing. A strong unity comes from affirming diversity in relation to similar goals. Homogeneity, in fact, impedes the possibility of unity because it is dogmatic and rigid and intolerant, and dogmatism and rigidity and intolerance have never been a basis for a vibrant unity.

The Political Intellectual

Interview by Anders Stephanson

Anders Stephanson: Philosophically speaking, you come out of the American tradition of pragmatism. In everyday parlance, pragmatism is often understood as adjusting in an almost opportunistic manner to existing circumstances. Philosophical pragmatism is something quite different.

Cornel West: When philosophers talk about pragmatism, they are talking about Charles Peirce, William James, and John Dewey. For me, it is principally Dewey. Three theses are basic: (1) anti-realism in ontology, so that the correspondence theory of truth is called into question and one no longer can appeal to Reality as a court of appeal to adjudicate between conflicting theories of the world; (2) anti-foundationalism in epistemology, so that one cannot in fact invoke non-inferential, intrinsically credible elements in experience to justify claims about experience; and (3) de-transcendentalizing of the subject, the elimination of mind itself as a sphere of inquiry. These three theses (mainly Dewey's) are underpinned by the basic claim that social practices—contingent, power-laden, structured social practices—lie at the very center of knowledge. In other words, knowledge is produced, acquired, and achieved. Here, the link to the Marxist tradition, especially that of Antonio Gramsci, looms large for me.

Q: These claims also have similarities with some poststructuralist theory.

West: Very much so. De-transcendentalizing the subject is, in Derrida's case, of course, a matter of the decentering of the subject, and in that regard his deconstruction clearly converges with Dewey's three basic theses of long ago. Derrida is more than a skeptical footnote to Husserl, but he can be viewed as that; and when he is, his deconstruction is a problematization of Husserl's quest for certainty within the interior monologue, within the self-presence of consciousness, within the mental theater.

Q: There is obviously no pragmatic agreement on what Derrida at times is erroneously understood to be arguing, the absurd idea that there is nothing outside the text.

West: He can actually be understood to claim that there is nothing outside social practices: intertextuality is a differential web of relations shot through with traces, shot through with activity. For a pragmatist, that activity is always linked to human agency and the context in which that agency is enacted. If he is read that way, I am in agreement.

Q: Poststructuralism is a critique of Marxism insofar as it undermines "the worldliness of the text"; but what also stands out is the attack on totalizing and totality. In the French context, this seems in part an effort to escape from Sartre's shadow, in part a general reaction against the postwar dominance of Marxism within the intelligentsia. In the "totalizing heterogeneity" of the United States one might well feel more inclined to retain some notion of totality.

West: I agree. Without "totality," our politics become emaciated, our politics become dispersed, our politics become nothing but existential rebellion. Some heuristic (rather than ontological) notion of totality is in fact necessary if we are to talk about mediations, interrelations, interdependencies, about totalizing forces in the world. In other words, a measure of synechdochical thinking must be preserved, thinking that would still invoke relations of parts to the whole, as for example the Gramscian articulation of spheres and historical blocs. It is true, on the other hand, that we can no longer hang on to crude orthodox "totalities" such as the idea of superstructure and base.

Q: It is curious that French poststructuralism in a way shares its fixation on language with Habermas, an antagonistic thinker thoroughly mired in "modernity." I find the idea of language as a model for social and political theorizing quite suspect.

West: Language cannot be a model for social systems, since it is inseparable from other forms of power relations, other forms of social practices. I recognize, as Gadamer does, the radical linguisticality of human existence; I recognize, as Derrida does, the ways in which forms of textualization mediate all our claims about the world; but the linguistic model itself must be questioned. The multi-level operations of power within social practices—of which language is one—are more important.

Q: This is why you describe yourself as a "neo-Gramscian pragmatist."

West: Gramsci's notion of hegemony is an attempt to keep track of these operative levels of power, so one does not fall into the trap of thinking that class relations somehow can be understood through linguistic models; so one does not fall into the trap of thinking that state repression that scars human bodies can be understood in terms of linguistic models. Power operates very differently in non-discursive than in discursive ways.

Q: The earlier Foucauldian distinction between discursive and non-discursive formations remains valid for you then?

West: He should have held on to it, just as Habermas should have held on to his earlier notion of interaction—a notion rooted in the marxist talk about social relations of production—rather than thinning it out into some impoverished idea of communication. Both can be seen as a move toward linguistic models for power.

Q: Even in the case of Foucault? His pan-power

theories are, after all, discursive rather than purely *linguistic*.

West: True. The later, genealogical Foucault would not make claims on linguistic models, but he remained more interested in power as it relates to the constitution of the subject than in power as such. Now, the structure of identity and subjectivity is important and has often been overlooked by the marxist tradition; but forms of *subjection* and *subjugation* are ultimately quite different from "thick" forms of oppression like economic *exploitation* or state *repression* or bureaucratic *domination*. At any rate, "the conditions for the possibility of the constitution of the subject" is a Kantian question to which there is no satisfactory answer. To answer it, as Heidegger said in his self-critique, is to extend the metaphysical impulse in the name of an attack on metaphysics. From that viewpoint, Foucault's notion of anonymous and autonomous discourses is but one in a series of attempts going back to Kant's transcendental subjects and Hegel's transindividual world spirits.

Q: What if Foucault would have said that he recognized the existence of other types of oppression but that his field of analysis was simply different?

West: I would have replied: "Fine, but that sounds more like the language of an academic than a political intellectual." It would have been to fall into the same traps of disciplinary division of labor he was calling into question. If, in fact, one is writing texts that are strategic and tactical in relation to present struggles, then it is difficult for me to see how one can be counter-hegemonic without actually including "thick" forms.

Q: At any rate, the poststructuralist problematic seems now to have been engulfed by the general debate on postmodernism. A certain confusion of terminology marks this debate. Conceptual pairs like modernity/postmodernity and modernism/postmodernism mean very different things depending on country and cultural practice.

West: Three things are crucial in clearing that up: historical periodization, demarcation of cultural archives and practices, and politics/ideology. Take history and demarcation for example. It is clear that "modern" philosophy begins in the seventeenth century, well before the Enlightenment, with the turn toward the subject and the new authority, the institutionalization, of scientific reason. What we call postmodern philosophy today is precisely about questioning the foundational authority of science. This trajectory is very different from that of modernist literary practices, which in turn is quite different from that of architecture: the former, to simplify, attacks reason in the name of myth, whereas the latter valorizes reason together with technique and form. These problems of periodization and demarcation are often ignored. For instance, Portoghesi's work on postmodern architecture seems to assume that his historical framework is an uncontroversial given.

Q: In this sense, Lyotard's initial theorization of the postmodern condition is profoundly marked by its French provenance.

West: Yes. His book, in many ways an over-celebrated one, is really a French reflection on the transgressions of *modernism* that has little to do with *postmodernism* in the American context. In France, modernism still appears to be the *centering* phenomenon. Figures like Mallarmé, Artaud, Joyce, and Bataille continue to play a fundamental role. In the United States, as Andreas Huyssen has emphasized, postmodernism is an avant-garde—like rebellion against the modernism of the museum, against the modernism of the literary and academic establishment. Note, too, the disjunction here between cultural postmodernism and postmodern politics. For Americans are politically always already in a condition of postmodern fragmentation and heterogeneity in a way that Europeans have not been; and the revolt against the center by those constituted as marginals is an *oppositional* difference in a way that poststructuralist notions of difference are not. These American attacks on universality in the name of difference, these "postmodern" issues of Otherness (Afro-Americans, Native Americans, women, gays) are in fact an implicit critique of certain French postmodern discourses about Otherness that really serve to hide and conceal the power of the voices and movements of Others.

Q: From an American viewpoint, the debate between Lyotard and Habermas is thus rather off-the-mark.

West: Interesting *philosophical* things are at stake there, but the politics is a family affair, a very narrow family affair at that. Habermas stands for the grand old tradition of the Enlightenment project of *Vernunft*. I have some affinities with that tradition, but there is nothing new about what he has to say. Lyotard's attack on Habermas comes out of a valorization of the transgression of modernism vis-à-vis an old highbrow, Enlightenment perspective. All this is very distant from the kind of debates about postmodernism we have in the States, though of course one has to read it, be acquainted with it.

Q: Agreed, but the debate has not been without effect here either. For instance, it is now often felt necessary in architectural discussions to make references to Lyotard.

West: It has become fashionable to do so because he is now a major figure, but I am talking about *serious* readings of him. Anyone who knows anything about Kant and Wittgenstein also knows that Lyotard's readings of them are very questionable and wrenched out of context. When these readings then travel to the United States, they often assume an authority that remains *uninterrogated.*

Q: A case in point is the concept of "life-world," now freely bandied about and most immediately originating in Husserl. In the later Habermas it fulfills an important function as the site of colonization for the "systems-world."

This, roughly, seems to combine Weber with Husserl, but the result is in fact nothing so much as classic American sociology.

West: When Habermas juxtaposes the life-world with the colonizing systems, it strikes me as a rather clumsy Parsonian way of thinking about the incorporation of culture into advanced capitalist cycles of production and consumption. On the one hand, Habermas has in mind the fundamental role that culture has come to play, now that the commodification process has penetrated cultural practices which were previously relatively autonomous; on the other hand, he is thinking of how oppositional forces and resistance to the system (what I call the process of commodification) are on the wane. This is simply a less effective way of talking about something that Marxists have been talking about for years.

Q: Yet, it is obvious that both Lyotard and Habermas must have done something to fill a kind of lack somewhere: otherwise their reception here would be inexplicable.

West: True. These remarks do not explain why Habermas and Lyotard have gained the attention they have. Habermas, of course, speaks with the status of a second-generation Frankfurt School theorist; and he has become such a celebrity that he can drop a number of terms from a number of different traditions and they take on a salience they often do not deserve. More fundamentally, his encyclopedic knowledge and his obsession with the philosophical foundations of democratic norms also satisfy a pervasive need for left-academic intellectuals—a need for the professional respectability and rigor that displace political engagement and this-worldly involvement. At the same time, his well-known, but really tenuous, relation to Marxism provides them with an innocuous badge of radicalism. All of this takes place at the expense of an encounter with the marxist tradition, especially with Gramsci and the later Lukács of the Ontology works. In this sense, Habermas unwittingly serves as a kind of opium for some of the American left-academic intelligentsia. The impact of Lyotard, on the other hand, is probably the result of the fact that he was the first serious European thinker to address the important question of postmodernism in a comprehensive way. Deleuze, to take a related philosopher, never did; though he is ultimately a more profound poststructuralist who should get more attention than he does in the United States. His early book on Nietzsche is actually an original text.

Q: Why?

West: Because Deleuze (and Levinas was the first to think through the notion of difference independent of Hegelian ideas of opposition, and that was the start of the radical anti-Hegelianism which has characterized French intellectual life in the last decades. This position—the trashing of totality, the trashing of mediation, the valorization of difference outside the subject-object opposition, the decentering of the subject—all these features we now associate with postmodernism and poststructuralism go back to Deleuze's resurrection of Nietzsche against Hegel. Foucault, already assuming this Deleuzian critique, was the first important French intellectual who could *circumvent*, rather than confront, Hegel, which is why he says that we live in a "Deleuzian age." To live in a Deleuzian age is to live in an anti-Hegelian age so that one doesn't have to come to terms with Lukács, Adorno or any other Hegelian Marxists.

Q: Nietzsche's ascendancy was not without maleficent effects when French theory was imported into the United States.

West: It was unfortunate for American intellectual life, because we never had the marxist culture against which the French were reacting. Nor was it a culture that took Hegel seriously: the early John Dewey was the only left Hegelian we ever had. Nietzsche was received, therefore, in the context of analytic philosophy, and you can imagine the gaps and hiatuses, the blindness that resulted when Nietzsche entered narrow Anglo-American positivism. In literary criticism, on the other hand, Nietzsche was part of the Derridean baggage that the "New Critics" were able easily (and often uncritically) to assimilate into their close readings. As a result, we now have a "Tower of Babel" in American literary criticism.

Q: The current, however, does not run in only one direction. Is the present French interest in "postanalytic" philosophy an indication that intellectual life is being reoriented toward the United States, at least in terms of objects of inquiry?

West: No doubt. French society has clearly come under the influence of Americanization, and West Germany, always somewhat of a fifty-first state, has moved in this direction as well. More immediately, now that the university systems in Europe no longer have the status or financial support they once had, American universities are pulling in the European intellectuals, offering money and celebrity status but also a fairly high level of conversation.

Q: Features of what we associate with the concept of postmodernism have been part of American life for a long time: fragmentation, heterogeneity, surfaces without history. Is postmodernism in some sense really the codification of life in Los Angeles?

West: Only in one form and specifically at the level of middlebrow culture. The other side is the potentially oppositional aspect of the notion. Postmodernism ought never to be viewed as a homogeneous phenomenon, but rather as one in which political contestation is central. Even if we look at it principally as a form of Americanization of the world, it is clear that within the US there are various forms of ideological and political conflict going on.

Q: The black community, for example, is more "contestational" than average America.

West: The black political constituency still has some

sense of the reality of the world, some sense of what is going on in the third world. Look at the issues Jesse Jackson pressed in 1984 and now in 1988, and you find that they were issues normally reserved for the salons of leftist intellectuals. Bringing that on television had a great impact.

Q: Yet, the black American condition, so to speak, is not an uplifting sight at the moment.

West: Not at all. There is increasing class division and differentiation, creating on the one hand a significant black middle class, highly anxiety-ridden, insecure, willing to be co-opted and incorporated into the powers that be, concerned with racism to the degree that it poses constraints on upward social mobility; and, on the other, a vast and growing black underclass, an underclass that embodies a kind of *walking nihilism* of pervasive drug addiction, pervasive alcoholism, pervasive homicide, and an exponential rise in suicide. Now, because of the deindustrialization, we also have a devastated black industrial working class. We are talking here about tremendous hopelessness.

Q: Suicide has increased enormously?

West: It has increased six times in the last decades for black males like myself who are between eighteen and thirty-five. This is unprecedented. Afro-Americans have always killed themselves less than other Americans, but this is no longer true.

Q: What does a black oppositional intellectual do in these generally dire circumstances?

West: One falls back on those black institutions that have attempted to serve as resources for sustenance and survival, the black churches being one such institution, especially their progressive and prophetic wing. One tries to root oneself organically in these institutions so that one can speak to a black constituency, while maintaining a conversation with the most engaging political and postmodernist debates on the outside so that the insights they provide can be brought in.

Q: That explains why you are, among other things, a kind of lay preacher. It does not explain why you are a Christian.

West: My own left Christianity is not simply instrumentalist. It is in part a response to those dimensions of life that have been flattened out, to the surface-like character of a postmodern culture that refuses to speak to issues of despair, that refuses to speak to issues of the absurd. To that extent I still find Christian narratives and stories *empowering and enabling.*

Q: What does it mean to a black American to hear that, in Baudrillard's language, we are in a simulated space of hyper-reality, that we have lost the real?

West: I read that symptomatically. Baudrillard seems to be articulating a sense of what it is to be a French, middle-class intellectual, or perhaps what it is to be middle class generally. Let me put it in terms of a formulation from Henry James that Fredric Jameson has appropriated: there is a reality *that one cannot not know.* The ragged edges of the Real, of *Necessity,* not being able to eat, not having shelter, not having health care, all this is something that one cannot not know. The black condition acknowledges that. It is so much more acutely felt because this is a society where a lot of people live a Teflon existence, where a lot of people have no sense of the ragged edges of necessity, of what it means to be impinged upon by structures of oppression. To be an upper-middle-class American is actually to live a life of unimaginable comfort, convenience, and luxury. Half of the black population is denied this, which is why they have a strong sense of reality.

Q: Does that make notions of postmodernism meaningless from a black perspective?

West: It must be conceived very differently at least. Take Ishmael Reed, an exemplary postmodern writer. Despite his conservative politics, he cannot deny the black acknowledgment of the reality one cannot not know. In writing about black American history, for instance, he has to come to terms with the state-sponsored terrorism of lynching blacks and so on. This is inescapable in black postmodernist practices.

Q: How is one in fact to understand black postmodernist practices?

West: To talk about black postmodernist practices is to go back to bebop music and see how it relates to literary expressions like Reed's and Charles Wright's. It is to go back, in other words, to the genius of Charlie Parker, John Coltrane, and Miles Davis. Bebop was, after all, a revolt against the middle-class "jazz of the museum," against swing and white musicians like Benny Goodman, who had become hegemonic by colonizing a black art form. What Parker did, of course, was to Africanize jazz radically: to accent the polyrhythms, to combine these rhythms with unprecedented virtuosity on the sax. He said explicitly that his music was not produced to be accepted by white Americans. He would be suspicious if it were. This sense of revolt was to be part and parcel of the postmodern rebellion against the modernism of the museum.

Q: To me, bebop seems like a black cultural avant-garde that corresponds historically to abstract expressionism in painting—the last gasp of modernism—on which indeed it had some considerable influence.

West: Certainly they emerge together, and people do tend to parallel them as though they were the same, but abstract expressionism was not a revolt in the way bebop was. In fact, it was an instance of modernism itself. Bebop also had much to do with fragmentation, with heterogeneity, with the articulation of difference and marginality, aspects of what we associate with postmodernism today.

Q: Aspects of the cultural dominant, yes; but these elements are also part of modernism. Surely one can still talk about Charlie Parker as a unified subject expressing inner *angst* or whatever, an archetypal characteristic of modernism.

West: True, but think too of another basic feature of postmodernism, the breakdown of highbrow and pop culture. Parker would use whistling off the streets of common black life: "Cherokee," for instance, was actually a song that black children used to sing when jumping rope, or, as I did, playing marbles. Parker took that melody of the black masses and filtered it through his polyrhythms and technical virtuosity, turning it into a highbrow jazz feature that was not quite highbrow anymore. He was already calling into question the distinction between high and low culture, pulling from a bricolage, as it were, what was seemingly popular and relating it to what was then high. Yet, I would not deny the modernist impulse, nor would I deny that they were resisting jazz as commodity, very much like Joyce and Kafka resisted literary production as commodity. In that sense bebop straddles the fence.

Q: The ultimate problem, however, is whether it is actually useful to talk about someone like Charlie Parker in these terms.

West: It is useful to the degree that it contests the prevailing image of him as a modernist. As you imply, on the other hand, there is a much deeper question as to whether these terms *modernism/postmodernism* relate to Afro-American cultural practices in any illuminating way at all. We are only at the beginning of that inquiry.

Q: Was there ever actually a mass black audience for bebop?

West: Yes, Parker's was the sort of music black people danced to in the 1940s. Miles's "cool" stage was also big in the 1950s with albums like "Kinda Blue," though it went hand in hand with the popularity of Nat King Cole and Dinah Washington.

Q: What happened to this avant-garde black music when Motown and Aretha Franklin came along?

West: It was made a fetish for the educated middle

class, principally, but not solely, the white middle class. In absolute terms, its domain actually expanded because the black audience of middle-class origin also expanded. But the great dilemma of black musicians who try to preserve a tradition from mainstream domestication and dilution is in fact that they lose contact with the black masses. In this case, there was eventually a move toward "fusion," jazz artists attempting to produce objects intended for broader black-and-white consumption.

Q: Miles Davis is the central figure of that avant-garde story.

West: And he crossed over with the seminal record *Bitches Brew* in 1970, accenting his jazz origins while borrowing from James Brown's polyrhythms and Sly Stone's syncopation. *Bitches Brew* brought him a black mass audience that he had lost in the 1960s—certainly one that Coltrane had lost completely.

Q: Crossover artists, in the sense of having a racially mixed mass audience, are not very numerous today.

West: No, but there are more than ever: Whitney Houston, Dionne Warwick, Lionel Richie, Diana Ross, and Anita Baker. Baker is a very different crossover artist because she is still deeply rooted in the black context. Michael Jackson and Prince are crossover in another sense: their music is less rooted in black musical traditions and much more open to white rock and so forth.

Q: In Prince's case it has to do with the fact that he is not entirely from a black background.

West: Still, he grew up in a black foster home and a black Seventh Day Adventist church, but in Minneapolis, which is very different from growing up like Michael Jackson in a black part of Gary, Indiana. Minneapolis has always been a place of cultural cross-fertilization, of inter-racial marriages and relationships. The early Jackson Five, on the other hand, were thoroughly ensconced in a black tradition, and Michael began his career dancing like James Brown. Now, he is at the center of the black-white interface.

Q: Prince never really played "black" music as one thinks of it. His music is "fused" from the start.

West: To be in a black context in Minneapolis is already to be in a situation of fusion, because the blacks themselves have much broader access to mainstream white culture in general. You get the same thing with other black stars who have come out of that place.

Q: Michael Jackson, by contrast, is now a packaged middle-American product.

West: A non-oppositional instance of commodification in black skin that is becoming more and more like candy, more radical than McDonald's, but not by much. It is watered-down black music, but still with a lot of the aggressiveness and power of that tradition.

Q: Music is *the* black means of cultural expression, is it not?

West: Music and preaching. Here, rap is unique because it combines the black preacher and the black music tradition, replacing the liturgical-ecclesiastical setting with the African polyrhythms of the street. A tremendous *articulateness* is syncopated with the African drumbeat, the African funk, into an American postmodernist product: there is no subject expressing original anguish here but a fragmented subject, pulling from past and present, innovatively producing a heterogeneous product. The stylistic combination of the oral, the literate, and the musical is exemplary as well. Otherwise, it is part and parcel of the subversive energies of black underclass youth, energies that are forced to take a cultural mode of articulation because of the political lethargy of American society. The music of Grandmaster Flash and the Furious Five, Kurtis Blow, and Sugar Hill Gang has to take on a deeply political character because, again, they are in the reality that the black underclass *cannot not know*: the brutal side of American capital, the brutal side of American racism, the brutal side of sexism against black women.

Q: I always thought rap was too indigenous a black form of expression to make it in the general marketplace. Run/DMC has proven me wrong on this.

West: Indeed. Run/DMC is as indigenous as you can get. Upper-middle-class white students at Yale consume a lot of Run/DMC.

Q: Yet, the constitutive elements of rap seemed to me too fixed for it to become a permanent presence on the crossover scene: more anonymous and less easily assimilated into existing white concepts of melody and structure. This, too, is probably wrong.

West: People said the same thing about Motown in 1961, the same thing about Aretha Franklin, who is about as organic as you can get. She is not as accepted by mainstream white society as the smoother and more diluted Warwick and Ross, but she *is* accepted. That, from the perspective of 1964-65, is unbelievable. The same thing could happen with rap music, since the boundaries are actually rather fluid. But it won't remain the same.

Q: Where will rap end up?

West: Where most American postmodern products end up: highly packaged, regulated, distributed, circulated, and consumed.

Q: Preaching, as you said, is obviously a cultural form of expression; but is it a specifically *artistic* form?

West: Sure. The best preachers are outstanding oral artists, performance artists. Martin Luther King, Jr. gave white America just a small taste of what it is to be an artistic rhetorician in the black churches. Tremendous gravity and weight are given to these artistic performances because people's *lives* hang on them. They provide some hope from week to week so that these folk won't fall into hopelessness and meaninglessness, so that they won't kill themselves. The responsibility of the black preacher-artist is, in that sense, deeply functional, but at the same time it entails *a refinement of a form* bequeathed to him by those who came before. Black preaching is inseparable here from black singing. Most secular black singers come out of the choir, and the lives of the congregation hang on how they sing the song, what they put into the song, how passionate, how self-invested they are. Preaching is just less visible to the outside as an art form because words uttered once don't have the same status as cultural products; but the black preachers are artists with a very long tradition.

Q: Since it does not lend itself to mechanical reproduction, preaching is also hard to destroy by turning it into a business. How is this artistic form of expression actually evaluated?

West: In terms of the impact the preacher has on the congregation. This impact can take the form of cantankerous response, or the form of existential empowerment, the convincing of people to keep on keeping on, to keep on struggling, contesting, and resisting.

Q: It is Kant's acrobat who intervenes constantly to transform an otherwise unstable equilibrium into another equilibrium.

West: Well put. Black sermonic practices have not received the attention they deserve. As a matter of fact, black linguistic practices as such need to be examined better because they add a lot to the American language.

Q: Black language creates a wealth of new words, which are then quickly picked up by the mainstream.

West: Usually with significant semantic changes. Stevie Wonder's "Everything is alright, uptight, out of sight" is a string of synonyms. *Uptight,* when I was growing up, meant smooth, cool, everything is fine. By the time it got to middle America, *uptight* meant anxiety-ridden, the inability of everything to be fine. Similar semantic shifts, though perhaps less drastic, take place with *chilling out, mellowing out,* and other black expressions. *Chilling out* meant letting things be, a sort of Heideggerian notion of *aletheia,* letting the truth reveal itself, letting it shine, letting it come forth.

Q: Given the social circumstances of which it is a product, black American language seems to me, on the outside, not to allow very easily for prevalent white orders of theoretical reflection.

West: It is a hustling culture, and a hustling culture tends to be *radically* "practicalist," deeply pragmatic, because the issue is always one of surviving, getting over.

Q: This, I imagine, demands some sharp linguistic twists for you.

West: I am continually caught in a kind of "heteroglossia," speaking a number of English languages in radically different contexts. When it comes to abstract theoretical reflection, I employ Marx, Weber, Frankfurt theorists, Foucault, and so on. When it comes to speaking with the black masses, I use Christian narratives and stories, a language meaningful to them but filtered through and informed by intellectual developments from de Tocqueville to Derrida. When it comes to the academy itself there is yet another kind of language, abstract but often atheoretical, since social theorizing is mostly shunned. Philosophers are simply ill-equipped to talk about social theory: they know Wittgenstein but not Weber, they know J.L. Austin but not Marx.

Q: Apart from the musician and the preacher, black culture exhibits a third artist of great importance: the athlete. There is enormous emphasis on aesthetic execution in black sports.

West: You can see this in basketball, where the black player tries to *style* reality so that he becomes spectacle and performance, always projecting a sense of self; whereas his white counterpart tends toward the productivistic and mechanistic. A lot of time, energy, and discipline also go into it but usually with a certain *investment of self* that does not express the work ethic alone. Ali was, of course, exemplary in this respect. Not only was he a great boxer, but a stylish one as well: smooth, clever, rhythmic, syncopated.

Q: Whence comes this emphasis on spectacle?

West: Originally, it derives from an African sense of pageantry, the tendency to project yourself *in performance* in a way so that you are at one with a certain flow of things. By "one," I do not mean any romantic kind of unity between subject and object or pantheistic unification with nature, but at one with the craft and task at hand. It is also to risk something. Baraka has spoken of the African *deification of accident,* by which he indicated the acknowledgment of risk and contingency: to be able to walk a tightrope, to be able to do the dangerous, and to do it well. But it is a form of risk-ridden execution that is *self-imposed.*

Q: Among the various black modes of cultural expression, pictorial art has not, with all due allowances for graffiti art, been much in evidence. The black middle class seems uninterested and so does the underclass: art as a practice is esoteric and largely without rewards.

West: Access to the kinds of education and subcultural circles is much less available to potential black artists. In addition to the racism in the avant-garde world, painting and sculpture are not as widely appreciated as they ought to be in black America. Therefore, pictorial black artists are marginal. They deserve more black support—and exposure.

Q: Beyond impediments of entry, is there not also some indigenous cultural element at work here? There are, after all, many black writers and dancers.

West: The strong, puritanical Protestantism of black religion has not been conducive to the production of pictures. For the same reason, there is a great belief in the *power of the word,* in literate acumen. In fact, writers are sometimes given too much status and become "spokespeople" for the race, which is ridiculous. Yet, there is an openness, diversity, multiplicity of artistic sensibility when developed and cultivated in the black community.

Realist modes of representation are, for example, not inherently linked to Afro-American culture. The pioneering artwork of Howardina Pindell, Emma Amos, Benny Andrews, and Martin Puryear are exemplary in this regard.

Q: It is a cliché to say that we live in a society of images, but we obviously do. Blacks watch more television than the average. Do they appropriate these images differently?

West: There is an element of scrutiny involved. The images have been so pervasively negative, so degrading, and devaluing of black people—especially of black women—that the process has always been one tied to some skepticism and suspicion.

Q: Images are seen through a skeptical racial grid?

West: A racial grid as transmitted from one generation to the next. This does not mean it is always critical. Think, for example, of all the Italian pictures of Jesus that hang in black churches at this very moment, pictures of Michelangelo's uncles when the man was actually a dark Palestinian Jew. Such images are widely accepted. But that particular one is, of course, different because it is sacred and therefore much more difficult to question. There is a much more critical attitude towards television. With the exception of the new phenomenon of the Cosby Show and Frank's Place, black folk are still usually depicted there as buffoons, black women as silly.

Q: Images of blacks are sometimes produced by blacks, as in many music videos. Those I have watched tend to be either sentimental ones about people yearning for the "right one" or highly charged ones featuring minutely choreographed movement.

West: You also find a lot of conspicuous consumption: a lot of *very* expensive cars, and furs, and suits, and so forth. The American dream of wealth and prosperity remains a powerful carrot, because television producers are aware of the reality that the black audience cannot

not know. Another big problem is the relation between black men and women. Different kinds of women are projected as objects of desire and quest, but they are downright white women, or blacks who look entirely white, or very light-skinned black women. Rarely do you find any longing for the really *dark* woman. And when a black woman is the star, she is usually yearning for a black man who is light—never a white man, but a black man who is light.

Q: Black culture is, of course, as sexist as the rest.

West: In a different way. The pressure on Afro-Americans as a people has forced the black man closer to the black woman: they are in the same boat. But they are also at each other's throat. The relation is internally hierarchical and often mediated by violence: black men over black women.

Q: Is it not more unabashedly sexist in its macho version? For even though popular culture as such is deeply infused with macho imagery, it seems to me that the black ditto is more *overtly* so.

West: Black society shows the typical range from the extreme machismo of any patriarchy to a few egalitarian relations. Nonetheless, what you say is probably true, and there are simply no excuses for the vicious treatment of black women by these men. Yet, interaction between the sexes in the black community is unintelligible without highlighting the racist and poverty-ridden circumstances under which so many blacks live. Machismo is itself a bid for power by relatively powerless and degraded black men. Remember, too, that the white perception here is principally informed by interracial relations between black men and white women, relations in which black machismo is particularly pronounced. There is also an *expectation* among large numbers of white folk that black men be macho, and black men then tend to fulfill that expectation. Those who do not are perceived as abnormal. A crucial part of this phenomenon is the question of sexual prowess: if you're not a "gashman," your whole identity as a black male becomes highly problematic. So, to a degree, the process is a self-fulfilling prophecy.

Q: There has been an extreme destruction of the family within the black underclass. Aside from the obvious causes, why is this?

West: Aside from the changes in society as a whole, developments like hedonistic consumerism and the constant need of stimulation of the body, which make any qualitative human relationships hard to maintain, it is a question of a breakdown in cultural resources, what Raymond Williams calls structures of meaning. Except for the church, there are few potent traditions on which one can fall back in dealing with hopelessness and meaninglessness. There used to be a set of stories that could convince people that their absurd situation was one worth coping with, but the passivity is now overwhelming. Drug addiction is only one manifestation of this: to live a life of living death, of slower death, rather than killing yourself immediately. I recently spoke at a high school in one of the worst parts of Brooklyn, and the figures were staggering: almost 30 percent had attempted suicide, 70 percent were deeply linked to drugs. This is what I mean by "walking nihilism." *It is the imposing of closure on the human organism, intentionally, by that organism itself.* Such nihilism is not *cute.* We are not dancing on Nietzsche's texts here and *talking* about nihilism; we are in a nihilism that is *lived.* We are talking about real obstacles to the sustaining of a *people.*

Q: Which is not quite how Nietzschean nihilism is normally conceived.

West: There are a variety of nihilisms in Nietzsche, and this is not so much one in which meaning is elusive, certainly not one with a surplus of meaning. What we have, on the contrary, is not at all elusive: *meaninglessness,* a meaningless so well understood that it can result in the taking of one's own life.

A World of Ideas

Interview by Bill Moyers

Moyers: You've been seen in some very unusual places for an intellectual: the storefronts and streets of Harlem, the shanty-towns of South Africa, one of the worst high schools in one of the worst districts in Brooklyn. Why? Those are so far from Princeton, so far from the ivory tower.

West: I understand the vocation of the intellectual as trying to turn easy answers into critical questions and putting those critical questions to people with power. The quest for truth, the quest for the good, the quest for the beautiful, all require us to let suffering speak, let victims be visible, and let social misery be put on the agenda of those with power. So to me, pursuing the life of the mind is inextricably linked with the struggle of those who have been dehumanized on the margins of society.

Moyers: One black intellectual said you make him uncomfortable with your ease out there on the street.

West: Certainly I have tried, on the one hand, to uphold the discipline of the life of the mind, but on the other hand, to keep track of other people's humanity, their predicaments and plights. I want to empathize and sympathize with them the best that I possibly can.

Moyers: Many Americans believe that a substantial portion of the black community in the inner cities is simply saying yes now to death, violence and hate. What do you find when you go there?

West: I do find a lot of meaninglessness and hopelessness, but at the same time I find people who are struggling, trying to survive and thrive under excruciating conditions. So the question becomes: how does one attempt to transform this meaninglessness and hopelessness into a more effective kind of struggle and resistance? It's a very difficult task, but there are many highly courageous people, working people, ordinary people, who are trying to hold on to meaning and value in a society that revolves more and more around the market mentality, the market ethos that permeates almost every sphere of this society.

Moyers: What does that ethos do to a community?

West: It makes it very difficult to hold on to non-market values, such as commitment in relationships, solidarity, community, care, sacrifice, risk, and struggle. Market values encourage a preoccupation with the now, with the immediate.

Moyers: The future is now.

West: That's exactly right. What that means then is people feel they no longer have to work or sacrifice. Why? Because the big money can be achieved right now. In the black community market activity is at its most pernicious and vicious right now in the drug industry. Young people want to make the easy buck now. In many ways they are mirroring what they see in society at large, what they see on Wall Street. It makes it very difficult for them to take, not only commitment and caring and sacrificing, but ultimately human life itself seriously. Profits become much more important than human life. What we see is a very cold-hearted mean-spiritedness throughout these communities. I think again it reflects so much of our own culture and civilization. It's quite frightening.

Moyers: You've been making a lot of speeches to young people in the high schools like those in Brooklyn, where the situation is fairly miserable. What do you say to those young people?

West: I tell them we live in a society that suffers from historical amnesia, and we find it very difficult to preserve the memory of those who have resisted and struggled over time for the ideals of freedom and democracy and equality.

Then I provide some historical background of people who displayed this kind of courage in its highest form—people like Martin Luther King, Jr., Michael Harrington, Ida B. Wells Barnett, and other freedom fighters. Then I move up to the present and talk about how many of their parents and brothers and sisters in some way extend that kind of tradition. And I ask the kids: "Are you going to be part of this tradition? What's going to happen to this tradition? How can we keep it alive? How can we keep it vital and vibrant?"

Moyers: You're suggesting that each one of them can matter, and yet they're living in communities where the institutions have broken down, where the family is fragmented; there's a kind of chaos all around them. Don't they need institutions that will nurture them? Institutions they can hold on to for the message of self-worth and self-determination to take hold?

West: Oh, very much so. In fact, when I talk about the historical leaders, I talk about the institutions that produced them—the families, the schools, the colleges, the churches, the synagogues, and the temples. It's true that many American families, neighborhoods, and associations are undergoing a kind of disintegration and decomposition, but it's not thorough. There are still some American families and some black families that are holding together. There are still some neighborhoods, black, white, brown and Asian, that are holding together.

Moyers: What do you tell them about how to signify?

West: They have to hope. They have to hold on to some notion that the future can be different if they sacrifice, if they fight, if they struggle. This is an old message. I learned this message in the black church years ago. I'm very much a product of a loving black family and a caring black church. And more than anything else, the church taught me the lesson of the cross. The only way to hope, to faith, to live is through the blood. The cross is a symbol of the impossible possibility, to use Karl Barth's language, the impossible possibility of holding on to faith, hope, and love in the kind of world in which we live, the kind of world in which blood is in fact always flowing.

Moyers: Once upon a time the church did provide that kind of lesson, it did provide that kind of community. But a poll I saw just recently said that in the black community, the church is less and less a part of the life of young people. Do you find that so?

West: The influence of the black church is declining as are churches around the country. But I do think that the message of the church remains relevant, even among those who are not Christians. The value of service to others, the value of caring for others, the value of attempting to keep one's eye on the forms of social misery, inadequate housing, health care, child care, unemployment and underemployment—religion has no monopoly on these kinds of values. Religion may help motivate persons to act on these values in light of the stories within their traditions, but neither Christians nor Jews nor Muslims nor Hindus have a monopoly on this.

Moyers: I've always been curious why so many blacks, when they were brought to this country, adopted Christianity, which was the religion that often defended the slavery that imprisoned them. How do you explain that?

West: I think large numbers of black people turned to Christianity for three basic reasons. The first had to do with issues of meaning and value. Black people arriving here 371 years ago had to come to terms with the absurd in the human condition in America, the place of enslavement.

Moyers: So that image of the Exodus, of the slaves freeing themselves, was especially appealing to black slaves in America.

West: Yes. The God of history who sides with the oppressed and the exploited, a God who accents and affirms one's own humanity in a society that is attacking and assaulting black intelligence and black beauty and black moral character, namely white supremacist ideology—this message spoke very deeply at the level of meaning and value. But Christianity is also important institutionally because black people appropriated primarily the left wing of the Reformation. The Baptists and the Methodists are much more democratically structured than the Catholics. The preachers are immediately accountable to the congregation, and the pew has access to leadership. Black humanity at the level of both leadership and followership could be accented.

Then I think there was also a political reason. Black people could engage in a form of critique of slavery, of Jim Crowism, of second-class citizenship, while holding on to the humanity of those who they opposed. This is the great lesson of Martin Luther King, Jr., who is a product of this tradition.

Moyers: We have opponents, but not enemies.

West: That's exactly right. Actually, the enemy is oppression and exploitation. It's legitimate to abhor and hate oppression and exploitation, but we cannot lose sight of the humanity of those who are perpetuating it. This is a very difficult and complex doctrine because it seems to promote a kind of a masochistic love of oppressor.

Moyers: The negative side of religion was that it could breed apathy and compliance. Also, the black church could even become a haven for charismatic con men, as modern-day television is to some evangelists.

West: Sure. I think Karl Marx's critique of religion as an impotent form of protest against suffering has an element of truth. Religion has tended to legitimize and to undergird forms of oppression precisely because it provided a critique that remained spiritual and had very little understanding of the social and economic and political conditions that were sustaining the oppression. At its best, religion can provide us with the vision and the values, but it doesn't provide the analytical tools. One doesn't look to the Bible to understand the complexity of the modern industrial and post-industrial society. It can give us certain insights into the human condition, certain visions of what we should hope for, but we also need the tools. They are found outside of religious texts and outside of religious sensibilities. We move to the social sciences for some handle on the maldistribution of resources and wealth and income and prestige and influence in our society. So all forms of prophetic religion must be linked in some sense with a set of analytical tools.

Moyers: But there is still in that old scripture a very powerful moral message. You end one of your books, *Prophecy Deliverance,* with a quote of Jesus from Luke 4:18: "The spirit of the Lord is upon me because he has anointed me to preach good news to the poor. He has sent me to proclaim release to the captives and recovering of sight to the blind, to set at liberty those who are oppressed." Do you think that message still means anything in urban areas where you visit often?

West: Yes, I do. I think it means that there is still someone who cares for those who are socially invisible and politically marginalized. The spirit of the Lord is still empowering to those who have been cast aside to struggle, enabling those who've been cast aside to not lose hope.

Moyers: You have been on a long intellectual odyssey yourself. Are you still an active Christian?

West: Very much so. Jesus' words, along with many others, have helped sustain me as I encountered for myself the absurdity of being both an American and a person of African descent. W.E.B. Du Bois talked about this years ago in his American classic *Souls of Black Folk.* "All that people of a darker hue have ever wanted to be," he said, "is human beings who could be both American and also acknowledge their African heritage." This double consciousness, of living in many ways *in* America but not still fully *of* it, is a tension, I think, that all of us forever grapple with. Those words allow me to hold on to my sense of possibility.

Moyers: You have talked about combative spirituality. What do you mean by that?

West: I mean a form of spirituality—of community and communion—that preserves meaning by fighting against the bombardments of claims that we are inferior or deficient. Combative spirituality sustains persons in their humanity but also transcends solely the political. It embraces a political struggle, but it also deals with issues of death or dread, of despair or disappointment. These are the ultimate facts of existence and they're filtered through our social and political existence. Ultimately all of us as individuals must confront these, and a combative spirituality accents a political struggle but goes beyond it by looking death and dread and despair and disappointment and disease in the face and saying that there is in fact a hope beyond these.

Moyers: But isn't that hope deferred again? Isn't that justice deferred? Isn't that saying, "You have to put up with the miserable conditions in Brooklyn today, in Harlem, because one day there'll be a reward?"

West: No, because it calls into question all illusions that there'll be a Utopia around the corner. When you talk about hope, you have to be a long distance runner. This is again so very difficult in our culture, because the quick fix, the overnight solution, mitigates against being a long distance runner in the moral sense, the sense of fighting because it's right, because it's moral, because it's just. That kind of hope linked to combative spirituality is what I have in mind.

Moyers: So combative spirituality is that sense of subversive joy, as you once called it?

West: Subversive joy is the ability to transform tears into laughter, a laughter that allows one to acknowledge just how difficult the journey is, but also to acknowledge one's own sense of humanity and folly and humor in the midst of this very serious struggle. It's a joy that allows one both a space, a distance from the absurd, but also empowers one to engage back in the struggle when the time is necessary.

Moyers: Some of that has come, has it not, from black music, from gospel and jazz and blues.

West: Yes.

Moyers: What about rap? Does rap have any of that spiritual energy in it?

West: Oh, very much so. I mean, black rap music is the most important popular musical development in the last ten years. It is a profound extension of the improvisational character of what I call the Afro-American spiritual blues impulse, which is an attempt to hold at bay the demons and devils. What rap has done is to allow a kind of marriage between the rhetorical and the musical by means of some of the most amazing linguistic virtuosities we have seen in the language, the lyrics, the quickness, the speaking.

Moyers: You have said that rap music is part and parcel of the subversive energies of the youthful black underclass. What do you mean by subversive energies?

West: They respond to their sense of being rejected by the society at large, of being invisible in the society at large, with a subversive critique of that society. It has to do with both the description and depiction of the conditions under which they're forced to live, as well as a description and depiction of the humanity preserved by those living in such excruciating conditions. It then goes beyond to a larger critique of the power structure as a whole. It is international in terms of its link to struggles in South Africa, so that in that sense it's part of a prophetic tradition. But I should say that what is lacking in rap music is vision and analysis. It's fun, it's entertaining, it helps sustain the rituals of party-going on the weekends, but it still lacks a vision. This is where again the church plays an important role, you see, because otherwise, it's quite easy to channel these energies into very narrow, chauvinistic, xenophobic forms that lack vision, that have no moral content or ethical substance.

Moyers: Blacks have made an enormous contribution in this country through preaching, through music, through sports, yet we still see the black underclass sinking in a quagmire. Almost every analyst I know says nothing is helping, not black rap music, not the black church, not social programs, not capitalist economics. Nothing is helping this black underclass. And yet you still trumpet hope.

West: Yes, I do. I mean, the condition of the black underclass is tragic, but they are still human beings who are getting about. Many are still making sense of the world. Many are actually still escaping. I don't want to lose sight of them. Many are still in churches trying to hold on to their moral character. Many are outside of churches trying to hold on to their moral character. I don't want to view the black underclass as a monolithic or homogeneous entity. These are actual human beings, children of God. Some are losing, many are losing, some are winning in terms of holding on to their sense of self and holding on to their sense of vitality and vibrancy.

That in no way excuses the structural and institutional forces that are at work: the unemployment, the failed educational system, the consumer culture that bombards them. The black underclass still has to contend with all of these in addition to the larger racist legacy. But it's not only about race. As we know, there are other factors as well. So that certainly a description of their conditions must include this, but I hold up hope. I'm talking about my cousins and friends and relatives who are seemingly locked into this condition, yet change can indeed come about.

Moyers: Where is the moral outrage in society today? Do you see it?

West: Not enough. There's been a kind of anaesthetizing, I think, in the 1980s toward forms of social misery. But there's the National Coalition of the Homeless.

There's the NAACP and DSA, Democratic Socialists of America, of which I'm an honorary chair. There's a whole host of groups that have been trying to sustain some moral outrage, filtered through a systemic analysis of our situation and regulated by a vision. It hasn't taken the way it has in past decades, but I think the 1990s will be different.

Moyers: The conundrum is that if you are morally outraged today, you're relegated to the margins of society. It's almost considered out of the norm to be concerned about social misery. To be mature today means you're supposed to say we can't ameliorate certain circumstances in life.

West: But I think the important point there is that we have to understand why this is so. Why has cynicism become so pervasive over the past ten years for those who wanted to focus on social misery? And I see that cynicism more and more on the wane. I think Eastern Europe is providing us with a different lesson, you see. Up until the last few months, people did not believe that ordinary human beings organized could fundamentally change society. We had scholars around the world saying that the very notion of revolution was outdated and antiquated. We could not even imagine a transfer of power that we have witnessed in Eastern Europe in the past month and a half. So all of those assumptions and presuppositions are now being called into question, which means that the focus of ordinary people organizing, mobilizing, having impact on powers that be, once again moves to the center of the agenda.

Part III
Toward Prophetic Action

Beyond Eurocentrism and Multiculturalism

I'd like to begin with two epigraphs.

The first is from that famous essay by Paul Valéry ("The Crisis of the Mind"), written in 1919—you probably know the first sentence by heart: "We later civilizations...we too now know that we are mortal." He goes on to say: "The idea of culture, of intelligence, of great works, has for us a very ancient connection with the idea of Europe...Other parts of the world have had admirable civilizations, poets of the first order, builders, and even scientists. But no part of the world has possessed this singular *physical* property: the most intense power of radiation combined with an equally intense power of assimilation." This is 1919, five years after August 1914. He goes on to say: "Everything came to Europe, and everything came from it. Or almost everything." (That's the wit that Adorno liked, when he called Valéry the exemplary cultural critic, as it were.) But he goes on to say: "Now, the present day brings with it this important question: can Europe hold its preeminence in all fields? Will Europe become *what it is in reality*— that is, a little promontory on the continent of Asia—or will it remain *what it seems*, that is, the elect portion of the terrestrial globe, the pearl of the sphere, the brain of a vast body?"

The second is from Frantz Fanon, a young man, 35 years old, who says, in *The Wretched of the Earth* (1961): "European nations sprawl, ostentatiously opulent. This European opulence is literally scandalous, for it has been founded on slavery, and it has been nourished with the blood of slaves and it comes directly from the soil and from the subsoil of that underdeveloped world. The well-being and the progress of Europe have been built up with the sweat and dead bodies of Negroes, Arabs, Indians, and yellow races." He concludes: "The wealth of the imperial countries is our wealth too...For in a very concrete way Europe has stuffed herself inordinately with the gold and raw materials of the colonial countries: Latin America, China and Africa. From all these continents, under whose eyes Europe today raises up her tower of opulence, there has flowed out for centuries toward that same Europe diamonds and oil, silk and cotton, wood and exotic products. Europe is literally the creation of the Third World. The wealth which smothers her is that which was stolen from the underdeveloped peoples."

Two starting points, two half-truths, as it were, both engaging in an excessive and extravagant rhetoric, but both reflecting on the contributions of an age that lasted from 1492 to 1945, let us call it the Age of Europe. We now live 46 years after the end of that Age of Europe, and we've yet to come to terms intellectually with the ramifications and repercussions of what it means to live in a world in which those nations between the Ural mountains and the Atlantic Ocean no longer sit at the center of the historical stage. The ambiguous legacy of that age confronts us, and, as Eliot reminds us, we don't inherit it, we obtain it by hard labor, we recast it, we reinterpret it, we reevaluate it in light of our present. What are the contributions?

One is the European construction of distinctive forms of historical consciousness that highlight the operations of powers and especially human powers, the human making and remaking that provides the fundamental challenge not simply to our philosophical claims but to our conception of ourselves. Hence, we discover the radical contingent character of whatever claims we put forward and the capacity of human beings to make and remake themselves and thereby make and remake history, and hence to project possibilities, both for the self and for society, for the individual, for individual individuality, which is not to be confused by discourses on the subject. In many ways, the French have suffocated philosophical debate by thinking that when you're talking about bodies and individuals you're some-how part of a subject's inner discourse; there's a whole host of ways of talking about individuals and bodies that don't have to go the subject-object route. My favorite: *The Quest for Certainty*; the Gifford lectures of '29, John Dewey, who, with no reference to subject-object dichotomies, still talks about individuality—unique, singular, irreducible bodies in search of the flourishing and flowering of their capacities and possibilities. This is inseparable from that new con-struction of historical consciousness that moves toward the center in nineteenth century Europe and begins to engage in its own transgressive acts vis-à-vis authority, especially, of course, the authority of the Church and the authority of kings.

The second contribution, the center of this transgres-sion, is the idea of democracy, the notion that these unique, singular, and irreducible bodies with these capacities and potentialities ought to—it's a normative claim—participate in decision-making processes and institutions that guide and regulate their lives. This is a subversive idea. And it's perennial, with self-correction and self-critique at its center. In many ways, the pragmatist tradition has been the distinc-tive philosophical tradition to make democracy not just a mode of governance but a way of being in the world, the fundamental object of its investigation. That's why Walt Whitman means much to Dewey, you see. Not too many others, besides Dewey and (at moments) Du Bois, have understood democracy in this deep sense.

Liberal debates tend to hold these contributions, tend to hold transgressive democracy, at arm's length, because historically "democracy" has depended on imperial condi-tions, not idealized forms. What are the conditions, the historical conditions, under which these liberal societies could emerge? Certain economic surpluses have been req-uisite for the social stability that has expanded liberal rights. That's why we need a theory-laden historiography. We know democracy is a good thing, we invoke it, and yet we need to see what Fanon saw, what my grandfather saw: a patriarchal "democracy" on the ground, with institutionalized terrorism and the strange fruit that Southern trees bear, the strange fruit Billie Holiday sings about. "Liberal society." From what vantage point? For whom? Those questions do not undermine the principles, but they perform a critique of the practices.

Reflections on the end of the Age of Europe, prompting these two questions, can help us move beyond the very, very limited and truncated debate about multiculturalism and Eurocentrism as the debate now rages in *Newsweek* and the *New Republic*. The response from the left must itself be self-critical, which means locating the larger layers of context on which this debate takes place, demystifying some of the categories that circumscribe the debate, then moving in a different direction that has to do with much more fundamental issues, issues that this debate is symptomatic of. With a nuanced historical sense, which evaluates the relation between the past and present, we can recognize ambiguous legacies, hybrid cultures, and heterogeneous populations across the board. Valéry put forward a half truth, and Fanon put forward a half truth. Half truths are dangerous, they mystify, they conceal, but they say enough about the real to seduce us. We have to talk about the present as history. We have to begin by situating our debate, which takes place at a moment—within our history as a country, nation, and empire—of economic decline and cultural decay. The sense of urgency, the ways in which issues of education and what academics these days call cultural production, has much to do with the economic decline and cultural decay that none of us can deny: the debt, the stubborn incapacity of the nation to mobilize resources requisite to provide necessary basic social goods, the short-term profiteering, the inability to provide education for a labor force, the inability to produce products of quality and quantity to compete with other countries, and most of all the cultural decay. The debate is about how we distribute social and cultural benefits, which is one of the functions of the university, of course. How are you going to distribute cultural/social benefits? Who gets in? Who teaches? Who has what status, prestige, what access to income?

We face the decomposition of civil society. We face shattered families, neighborhoods, civic associations—a shattering that is the distinctive feature of an empire in decline, as William McNeil has pointed out. We face the social breakdown of nurturing systems for children (not just their bodies but their souls), and hence deracinated individuals, rootless individuals, denuded individuals, culturally naked individuals who have lost their existential moorings, who become easily caught within a subculture of violence.

This is one national, one social, context in which the debate emerges. And then, what DeSousa and others are responding to is the impact of the new social history that enables us to see the relation between this present and the past. The new social historians, even given their own silences and blindnesses, are winning the day; they are thoroughly influential in terms of how humanists think about the past and present, how literary critics think about the past and present, even how philosophers think. Slices of humanity, subaltern and subjugated peoples, had been erased by intellectual elites who were hegemonic within the historical profession and who could only focus on the agency of certain kinds of human beings: military elites, political elites, well-to-do men. This revolution in historiography, especially given the historical turn in humanistic studies and in philosophy, has put the intellectual right on the spot. It's not a matter of the new left, or the ex-new left, running the universities, as the *Commentary* crowd would have us think. It's a matter of history, and the fear of a history that can no longer be ignored: women's history, Afro-American history. If you're still talking about American culture and not talking about ways in which the institution of slavery was constitutive of the empire, then you're writing history in the way they wrote it in the 1940s and the 1950s. It has nothing to do with the historical weight and gravity of particular persons who performed particular roles that allowed for the possibility of the emergence of the major empire in the middle part of the twentieth century: the American Empire.

Given these breakthroughs, we have a *kulturkampf* within the academy. But we need to keep in mind that this is only a slice of the professional, managerial strata in American capitalist society. It's not the center of the universe. And this *kulturkampf* is being shaped by the very process of rationalization Max Weber talked about long ago, a process recast under new conditions, a new logic of professionalization, a reward structure geared toward research (and away from teaching), a highly bureaucratized space—namely: universities. Struggles over turf, slots, curriculum, and debates over multiculturalism have been reduced to the either/or option of the bureaucratic squabble. I'm suspicious of the framework, and I do not begin with the categories trotted out in *Newsweek*, the *New Republic*, and other middle-brow journals, nor with the categories trotted out by ex-Reagan technocrats such as DeSousa.

So, the first question I raise is: where does the term "Eurocentrism" come from? And where does "multiculturalism" come from? Is Eurocentrism synonymous with the Age of Europe? The very idea of Europe itself demands interrogation. It's too often unquestioned. We need to tell a story about ways in which "Eurocentrism" as a category for the debate is hiding and obscuring something, obfuscating a debate, prepackaging a debate that thereby never really takes place and becomes, instead, this battle between bureaucrats over slots and curriculum. You notice nobody's really raising issues of what it means to read a text critically; instead the issue is what text will "make it in." There are ways of reading Shakespeare and Dante that can be quite illuminating and profound, and ways of reading Toni Morrison that are flat. I want to know how people are reading these texts, and what kind of historical sense they have? Are they just occasions for cathartic expressions of identity? Just moments for the building up of a self-confidence that has been undermined by palpable white supremacist and male supremacist forces? This may be morally justifiable, but it is not intellectually justifiable. It's intellectually debilitating. That's why I begin with Valéry, because the only way we get beyond a paralyzing either/or perspective is to take a look at this idea of Europe, the very idea of Europe as an ideological construct. We need to look at Denys Hay's book of 1957—*Europe: The Emergence of an Idea*—and Henri Perinne's point that Charlemagne is inconceivable without Mohammed, that Europe as a noun is called forth by the caliphs, the Arab caliphs. For what? Imposed unity. The first time Europe was used as an adjective occurs in 1458, by Pius II, five years after the Turkish takeover of Constantinople. As a long story, this can begin to demystify "Europe."

Then, we need to tell the story of how literary figures—especially Matthew Arnold, based on his hero, Goethe—try to constitute a federation of European unity in the world of letters *because* it has never existed on the ground. Ironically, the right wing trots out Thomas Sterns Eliot as the exemplary Eurocentric critic, which he is, but *The Wasteland* is one of the most powerful critiques of the very notion of Europe at the center of the world, juxtaposing Europe with vegetation rites and Buddhism and Hinduism. Besides, Europe is always already multicultural; after Napoleon, multinational; after August 1914, involved in a series of "civil wars," nationalist clashes. Fifty million dead in 1945, with this idea of Europe demonizing Jews, part of a history of demonization that serves to protect this idea, this fragile construction. The Enlightenment bandwagon has wed itself to a notion of universalism and internationalism that never was, and that is, more than ever, over, in light of the decolonization of the Third World, which has unleashed new conceptions of identity that should make us suspicious of any glib notion of universality.

There is no way back to those Enlightenment conceptions of universality and cosmopolitanism. Now, I want to
hold on to universality, but I know it must now be imma-
nent, it's got to go down—very, very deep down—far
enough that it makes human connection. If it doesn't make
human connection, there will be parochialism, provincialism, narrow particularism, all linked of course to jingoism
and xenophobia. It's no accident that our moment is a
tribalistic moment, a xenophobic moment, not just in Eastern Europe, but in Chicago, in New York, parts of the Third
World, the Middle East. The quest for identity is fundamental. The quest for community is basic. For what? Protection,
meaning, value, the means by which human beings are
willing to face their extinction, with a sense of significance.
If the Left cannot talk to issues of identity and community in
such a way that it provides human connection, then there
will be no Left in the older sense of that term, in terms of
coalition and alliance, because I don't consider identity politics *ipso facto* left at all; those politics amount primarily to a
mode of middle class entrée.

This is why, again, in looking at the debate over multiculturalism, I recognize the degree to which it's very much
a middle class affair—very much a scrabble and scramble
over various kinds of resources within one particular slice
of our society. I don't want to downplay it, I don't want to
devalue it, but I think we have to situate it and see it for
what it is. And I think relations of universalism and particularism, objectivism and relativism, don't provide us the
tradition, or set of traditions, to see the debate for what it is.
Feminism has begun to help, I think, and certain intellectuals of color tried to help, but even our C.L.R. Jameses and
even our Du Boises themselves are very much part of an
older Enlightenment project, even though they were forced
to deal with particularity, even though they have moments
of profound insight. When C.L.R. James said "I am a European Black man," he recognized how thoroughly he had
been assimilated into an Enlightenment tradition in which

his own sense of identity was not at the very center.

The aim is—and this is what takes us back to Dewey again, you see—the aim is not giving up on universality, not giving up on threadbare notions of objectivity, not giving up on notions of balanced analysis, so it's not reduced simply to partisanship, it's not reduced solely to power struggle. There is space for critical exchange, but only if we acknowledge that truth has only a negative function, if we never reduce truth claims to assertability claims, if we recognize that all truths have a small 't,' if we recognize that truth with a big 'T' is always a fish that stands outside our conceptual net. Pragmatists have taught us that if truth is a species of the good, and the good is defined in terms of temporal consequences, then the universe is unfinished, and history is incomplete, and given that temporal dimension of knowledge claims, you can never claim that Truth, capital 'T,' has been arrived at. All you can say is small 't' revisable, as Quine puts it, not immune to revision. Small 't' provisional. And it's true for knowledge claims across the board. And this is very important, it seems to me, because there is a danger in reducing the talk about knowledge solely to a talk about power, just as there's a danger in talking about knowledge as if it's not linked to power.

To come to a conclusion here, let me say a word about politics because I actually believe, like Dewey, that democratic practices are themselves deeply rooted in precisely the nuanced historical sense, the subtle social analysis, and the self-correction and self-critical process of never blocking the road to inquiry. Democratic practices themselves are not just transgressive in an avant-gardist sense of shocking a bourgeois audience and so forth like Stravinsky and others; they are transgressive in the sense of fundamentally getting at the redistribution of power and wealth. Democracy is a difficult concept for Americans because we live in a very conservative society, which operates in part on economic growth by means of corporate priorities, and the disproportionate influence of big business, and which is also a chronically xenophobic society, in which the very conception of itself as a nation, as having a national identity, is rooted in a discourse of negatively-charged blackness and positively valued whiteness. That's our history. Now, we've had some great strugglers, John Brown and on and on and on. But our history means you can easily push that button to sustain the status, power, and privilege of particular outlooks and interests, especially the interests of big business. And that button is pushed over and over again: as with Willie Horton. Jesse Helms pushed it in North Carolina, I know it's been pushed many times in Chicago. And there's not only one kind of xenophobia, because of course it's deeply patriarchal as well as deeply homophobic. All societies and civilizations that we know have their own kind of xenophobia, and so it's not a matter of pointing the finger solely at the United States. But in the United States, because we think we enjoy democratic politics, this xenophobia makes it especially difficult for democratic politics to get off the ground. The best we do is produce social movements. But, then again, there cannot be significant social movements if there's no understanding of universalism, no understanding of an internationalism that digs deep, makes connections, makes coalition, and makes alliance. This is not an issue of the life of the mind. The point is that if you view yourself as part of a tradition of freedom fighting, and if you do view yourself as part of those whose backs are against the wall, and you're actually willing to live and die for that struggle, then forms of intellectual weaponry become crucial, and understanding what you're up against can become a question of life and death. Hence, Marx and Weber and Lukács and Simmel and Du Bois and Simone de Beauvoir become crucial means to stay on a slippery tightrope. And thank God that this tradition has some salience. The real danger is that traditions of freedom fighting will slowly but surely wane in our culture of consumption, and the very possibility of a different future, the very possibility of a sense of hope for a society that's better than the present will slowly but surely wane. In that kind of society, I'm not willing to live.

Interview

Bill Brown: Your talk suggests that Eurocentrism and multiculturalism, as two political positions within today's academy, aren't nearly so antagonistic as we might think. That antagonism takes place within an overarching mystification that we need to overcome, to move beyond or beneath.

Cornel West: That's right. The first move must be one of demystification, calling into question the prevailing myths perpetrated by both the so-called Eurocentric crowd and the so-called multiculturalist crowd. The crude Eurocentrists want to argue that Europe is some monolithic and homogeneous entity, with a tradition over time and space that demands unequivocal and uncritical acceptance. The crude multiculturalists want to argue that Europe is monolithic and homogeneous in the negative sense, and this position is just as sophomoric. Both positions perpetuate the ideological, fictive, mythic construct of "Europe," imposing a unity that never existed. Part of the problem is that crude Eurocentric figures, Lynn Cheney, and crude Multiculturalists, Leonard Jeffries within the Afrocentric crowd, share a monumentalist conception of culture. They're looking at the peaks of the past; they're looking for the great monuments of the past, a pyramid in Egypt or a Shakespeare. I don't want to downplay great achievement—the pyramid is fascinating—but I want to complicate it: those pyramids were based on the labor of thousands and thousands of persons suffering within a society dominated by the pharaoh. A monumentalist conception of culture needs to be radically called into question. And of course we need to oppose essentialist readings in which one side has all the monuments and the other has none, those readings that feed into the most vulgar kind of superiority claims about a race or a culture.

Now, I don't support sophomoric relativism. I am a radical democrat; I am a proponent of individuality in terms of the uniqueness, the irreducible and irreplaceable character of individuals shaped by groups and communities; so I do in fact want to argue that certain cultures—to the degree to which they conform to radical democratic principles and radical libertarian principles—are preferable to other kinds of cultures. I think a society under Mandela in South Africa would be morally preferable to what we have now in South Africa. So it's not a matter of "anything goes." I believe in contextualism, which is not the same thing as relativism, but which tries to understand ways in which various values and attitudes over time and space ought to be understood in relation to their respective context. This is an appreciation of the difference of human beings responding to different circumstances. That does not mean that anything goes, that any culture has the same value as any other culture. For me, you know, the subordination of women and workers and people of color is a fundamental issue having to do with democratic politics and having to do with human dignity that's worth fighting and dying for.

BB: Of course, while we're demythifying a monumentalist Europe, the fiction of Europe, we need to respect the power that fiction has had, the power of the imaginary difference between Europe and Africa, say. As Castoriadis has argued about nations, they may be imaginary but they lead to war.

CW: That's right. That's the work that the subtle social analysis has to do, and that's why the most important category for me, in terms of understanding the broad historical sweep, is "empire." It's empire. This is one of the reasons why someone like a Geoffrey Barraclough or even an Eric Voegelin is very important to me: they understand the past in terms of the constitution of empire, and the emergence, development and decline of empires, the clashing of empires. But imperial conquest takes place not simply over markets and raw materials, but also over cultural identities, cultural resources and languages. So you're right: when we talk about demystifying Europe, we're actually introducing analyses of power in which imperial conquests and subjugation of peoples of color in various ways are basic to the making of the Modern. The Modern is not reducible to just that, but we know it is basic for the constitution of what we understand the Modern to be.

BB: I'm interested in the present fate of "Multiculturalism" as a concept. Of course, according to the Right, the word marks a moment of decadence within the academy, the decline and fall from the universal, the essential, the non-political values. But by now the Left, certainly you yourself, have become suspicious about the term. Some people are arguing that multiculturalism is deployed prophylactically, enabling a department or university to point to its multicultural curricula in order to protect itself from significant contact with minorities, from hiring minorities. More simply, a multiculturalist agenda can simply produce "race," "gender," "ethnicity" as objects of knowledge to be consumed comfortably...without engagement.

CW: I'm ambivalent about the term. It's the language of bureaucrats. I recognize that I have to do battle at times under the banner of "multiculturalism" because of the nature of the attack and assaults on it from what we can call loosely "the Right." At the same time I don't want to accept "multiculturalism" because it seems to me to be an obscuring term, obscuring the deeper intellectual issues, such as what role professors play as cultural managers or cultural supervisors over the textual productions of any group. That's true whether that group is all black or all women or all gay or all lesbian. The same relations of power are actually at work, but they tend to be con-

cealed under the banner of "multiculturalism." The serious intellectual work mustn't stop once multiculturalism
becomes institutionalized and we have courses in black
writers and women writers and so on; we need the same
kind of critiques that have been brought to bear on the
earlier, more xenophobic canons.

BB: An institutionalized multiculturalism can look
like a version of exoticism, or of the sort of primitivism
that "saved" Western art in its modernist moment.

CW: Right. The exotic is a tradition that won't go
away, and it has to be interrogated over and over again.
It's a way for students and teachers to feel good about their
sense of liberal openness by being open to those who are
exotic, primitive, and so forth...to feel as if these people—
and when I say "these people" I include myself—are closer
to reality than was Shakespeare, Dante, Milton—to feel
as if these people are more authentic.

BB: Cornel West, the authentic Black man!

CW: Exactly! Speaking for all black men. Somehow
closer to the ground, more earthy, closer to the real. That's
a joke. Anybody who knows me knows that's a joke.

BB: Given the limitations of the debate, then, and
given the problems that remain even as we imagine multiculturalism moving from the margins to the center of
institutional concern, I'm wondering what step you pro-
pose. How do you reframe the debate to think about
canons and cultures differently? What does the new frame
look like?

CW: I think that the next step ought to be a candid
intellectual exchange over clashing conceptions of cultural citizenship. And by cultural citizenship I mean not
just the skills and techniques requisite to be an effective
speaker and doer in our society, but also the kinds of
intellectual traditions that ought to inform what it means
to be an active citizen in the American empire in the latter
part of the twentieth century, and specifically democratic
sentiments at the center of this understanding of cultural

citizenship. How do we foster critical sensibilities that are attuned to the relative lack of accountability mechanisms for elites? There are going to be elites—Pareto was right—there are going to be elites. The question is what kind of accountability mechanisms are in place.

What's fascinating about this next step is that the question becomes not so much what particular figures are trotted out that constitute a canon...who are the greatest hits of the West, the way in which Cheney and Bennett and company want it. The question becomes: how do you critically read whatever texts come before you, canonical or non-canonical, at the rhetorical level, and at the political level, in terms of the ways in which certain kinds of political sentiments are shot through these rhetorical enactments, and in terms of the particular conditions under which these texts were produced, distributed, and received. When you raise the issue to the level of cultural citizenship, democratic sentiments, and critical orientation, you can see how sophomoric the Cheney-Bennett view is, because the texts that they invoke, from Plato to Arnold, can subvert the Cheney-Bennett ideals.

In addition, there is much to learn from the silences in these texts. Toni Morrison has done wonderful work, as you know, on the unspeakable things unspoken—namely, the silences in the works of a Henry James or a Faulkner or a Hemingway, in texts in which black people are not major characters, but in which blackness is employed as a metaphor to sustain the narrative. There is a presence of *blackness* that makes those texts what they are. You can't run to a particular tradition of Afro-American literature and think that somehow there you're getting all the blackness in American literature, without reading *To Have and Have Not*, without seeing the crucial role that blackness plays as a metaphor, be it signifier of the id, or of chaos, or whatever. Bellow is the same way, my God, you know: the various metaphors that depend on blackness in Bellow are fundamental. That's the kind of level of analysis that it seems to me we ought to be moving toward if we're talking about new conceptions of cultural citizenship.

BB: Not surprisingly, this sounds a little like Dewey.

CW: Yes, that's true...even though Dewey didn't push it far enough.

BB: I mean the Dewey who emphasizes education, the dynamics of education, or education as dynamism. In *Democracy in Education,* you don't find "democracy" as a value to be located in Aristotle or Paine; you find democracy understood as an educational process, and education as a democratic process.

CW: I think you've pegged something that remains in some ways underdeveloped within my own thinking about what I'm doing. Even in my treatment of Dewey in *American Evasion,* I don't spend time trying to discern his understanding of the democratic process within the pedagogical arena that spills over into the larger conception of what it is to be a citizen in American society. I've just read Robert Westbrook's book on *John Dewey and American Democracy*—what a wonderful book that is—and he spends much time talking about the way in which Dewey understood democracy, using the pedagogical arena as one particular example of how one thinks democratically. I have to do more thinking and writing about this, but it seems implicit in what I've been saying.

BB: I think so. And what I'm imagining, with your idea about democratic citizenship (which I'd like to think of as the ongoing educative process), is that some of these ideas could be used to formulate a response to complaints, such as Elizabeth Fox Genovese's, that, in rethinking the canon, we're "sacrificing the ideal of collective identity." Not common texts, but a common approach to texts, a common responsibility, might serve this ideal...if it's an ideal worth serving.

CW: That's exactly right, and I think it cuts much deeper than what I construe as the static notions of a "common culture." I'm all for collective action and for civil intellectual exchange, but I am suspicious of the notion of common culture, not only because it has been used in conservative ways, but it presupposes a certain static consensus that any radical democrat is suspicious of, and that's true for a Jefferson or an Emerson as it's true for a Dewey or a Randolph Bourne or a Fannie Lou Hamer. These claims of common culture and commonality we have to be highly suspicious of. That doesn't mean, though, that we don't accent certain common processes to which we as individuals are responding—I mean, for example, capital accumulation, a common process that is now global, that we all respond to in some way relative to our histories, relative to our class positions, relative to our cultural heritages and so forth. When I talk about commonality, it has to do much more with capital accumulation, bureaucracy, communication networks...Those are common processes.

BB: They're the universal.

CW: Yes. That's what is universal, rather than this "common culture" that tends to hide certain elite bids for power that we've seen in the past.

BB: Du Bois, I'd say, believed in an essential African-American consciousness, not a universal African-American consciousness...

CW: No...

BB: ...but a consciousness arising from a shared history, the shared fate of the black man and the black woman in American political, economic, social history. Could we, thinking through the topic of the conference, call this something like the "nominal essence" of the African-American, as opposed to any real essence. "Nominal essence" is the phrase Teresa de Lauretis has used to rethink "essentialism," at the close of the 80s, in the feminist context.

CW: I'm suspicious of any form of essentialism, but, for example, I do believe a common denominator of white supremacist abuse cuts across class, gender, sexual orientation...in the New World. To that degree, "nominal essentialism" would be the inescapable fact of having to respond to some form of white supremacist abuse...black child, black woman, black man, black working man, black well-to-do woman, and so forth. It's fluid and protean, but it's an undeniable and inescapable fact; it's the same in terms of the commodification of labor for any human being in a capitalist society. It's inescapable, it conditions the way in which one goes about trying to promote one's life chances and to live one's life. If that's what we mean by "nominal essentialism," then I think the term's absolutely acceptable, very much so. It has nothing to do with identity, though. Essentialism has usually been linked to a discourse on identity, and this is where Black Nationalists, especially the more narrow ones, fall into essentialist traps, where they think that somehow the inescapable fact of white supremacist degradation will generate one particular response from people of African descent. That seems to me politically naive and intellectually indefensible.

BB: In your talk, you spoke of American "economic decline and cultural decay" as the context in which the debate over Eurocentrism and multiculturalism is now taking place. Is this decay what accounts for the Right's vociferous attack within the field of culture, for the emergence of concern about political correctness, for the National Association of Scholars? A debate over the canon seems trivial, given the Right's massive success in the political and economic arenas.

CW: We're dealing with ways in which one tries to come to terms with the escalating social chaos in the American empire. Conservatives at their worst are simply scapegoating the relatively powerless peoples—gays, lesbians, people of color, women—as the source of the cultural decay. Now for me the cultural decay is a fact. You know, a lot of my progressive colleagues and comrades wouldn't want to use that kind of language, but when I look at escalating homicides and suicides, the indices of social anomie, they are escalating, and they show a collapse of meaning and value and hope and love. That for me is a sign of decay. We're talking about the massive breakdown in the nurturing systems of children in a market-driven society that produces denuded and deracinated individuals with very little existential moorings or cultural apparatuses to deal with the abyss and the absurd. Once that occurs—and this has occurred historically in the collapse of various empires—then people must respond, and the Right wants to respond, so they look to the breakdown of the family and blame women, they look to neighborhoods and blame black people, they look to the schools and blame us Leftists.

BB: It's easier to blame people than to blame the system.

CW: What they won't highlight is the degree to which corporate activity, preoccupied with commodifying anything it can get its hands on, reinforces market values, a market mentality, and a spiritual impoverishment that characterizes so much of the American landscape these days. But the Left suffers because it really doesn't have a developed tradition of thinking about crucial cultural institutions in civil society—like family, or like neighborhood, or like church/synagogue/mosque. Feminists, I think, can talk profoundly about the family, not so profoundly about the neighborhood or religious institutions. The Left has perpetually found itself intellectually paralyzed in terms of the cultural crisis.

BB: It's difficult not to ask about juxtaposing your account of the American empire, that empire's decay, and the accounts of America's triumph, capitalism's triumph in Eastern Europe. Stuart Hall, as early as 1986, said that postmodernism amounts to everyone, everywhere, wanting to be "American." Now that's a postmodernity and a universality we've watched intensify in the last five years; that's a desire, according to *one* end-of-history thesis, that's now being satisfied.

CW: That's a good question, because we've seen the economic disintegration and slow but sure political collapse of the other great empire, the Soviet empire. It was the last barrier to the globalization of capital that imposed some constraints on this "Americanization" of the world, to use a very, very loose phrase. The globalization of capital will more than likely result in the "Latin Americanization" of Eastern Europe. For understandable reasons—the colossal failure of command economies, the immoral character of the repression and regimentation of populations—the 1990s have seen the accenting of the *libertarian* aspects of the modern period, from 1776 to 1989, the libertarian aspects of those bourgeois revolutions that have fundamentally shaped how we understand our freedom to speak and worship. We tend to accent those libertarian aspects, but to downplay those *egalitarian* aspects of revolutionary events in the modern world, from 1776 to 1974 in Angola, let's say, because that's what's most dangerous. Those egalitarian aspects foreground basic social goods—like health care and education and housing and food and employment. What's most dangerous, in the midst of the nationalist frenzy which is surfacing with the collapse of the Soviet empire, is that nationalist elites, as we've seen since the time of Napoleon, will try to impose their will on populations, fully suppressing the egalitarian ideals. Nationalism, intertwined with fundamentalism, intertwined with certain kinds of anti-Westernization aims, yet mediated by Western techniques and technologies—these cultural phenomena, I'd want to say again, are what the Left finds it difficult to understand even as the Left traditions are indispensable in terms of acknowledging how the globalization of capital is fundamental in shaping and spawning these cultural phenomena. Religious fundamentalism, nationalism—we know these have always been fanned by elites within nation-states in order to create some identity, to sustain social stability and order. Eric Hobsbawm's effort to make sense of nationalism is both inspiring and frustrating: he doesn't have the tools that deal with the deeper issues of identity and community, but he's isolating something very important, which is that there's always an excessive bourgeois appropriation of nationalist ideology.

BB: This limitation of the Left position—or, let's say, one traditional position on the Left—would seem to account for the reemergence of a populist discourse.

CW: Christopher Lasch.

BB: Christopher Lasch trying to transcend the right-left, reactionary-radical dichotomies.

CW: That's exactly right. It doesn't work, but it's a gallant attempt, it seems to me. I'd have to say more about Lasch's work on many different fronts, but for now I'd say it's symptomatic of trying to hold on to a critique of capitalist civilization—let's use those terms together—without being equipped to engage in a discourse on culture that keeps track of those who are subjugated, such as women. He wants to be a critic of capitalist civilization, and it's a very difficult thing to do, and none of us pull it off. But, certainly, he would be one example, among many others, of the effort to come up with a discourse that's critical of capitalist civilization that does keep track of family, and neighborhood, and religious institutions, and ecology, and so on.

BB: In part, the issue here is producing something more than critique, more than negative dialectics; in other words, imagining alternative cultural formations.

CW: A profound critique should provide some insights as to how you go about constituting and forming culture, and, on the other hand, as you constitute and form culture, you have to have the critique going along with it, so you don't end up with some kind of romanticized or idealized conception of some exotic culture. Here again, this is where the people of color and the discourse of otherness comes in, you know—"well, they've got the vital culture, hey let's go see what's going on there"—you get hip-hop music or whatever. Critique has to be relentless because within those cultural formations there are all kinds of homophobic and patriarchal elements that can be overlooked in the name of supporting a vital culture.

BB: Certainly your work on the African-American prophetic tradition, the role of religion in your own thinking—the populist strain, one might say—provides an alternative to typical Leftist critique.

CW: At times, out of sheer desperation, I look for prophetic energies that flow through black ecclesiastical institutions, prophetic black churches, prophetic black church women, prophetic black church men, to bring some form of radical democratic critique to American capitalist civilization *and* to imagine it embodied in everyday lives of ordinary people, in the form of sustainable institutions and infrastructures. That's what I'm always grasping for. At times I probably make exaggerated and extravagant claims in this regard, out of sheer desperation. But I do think, when we look at the historical past and present, we actually do see those voices and bodies on the margins of a black church tradition and that has perennially attempted to throw out both leaders, visions, followers, perspectives that keep alive some sense of critique and resistance to American capitalist civilization. I attempt not just to bring the critique to bear, as you were noting, in a negative way, but to talk positively about what is out there that holds a particular tradition together no matter how feeble or how defensive. There are these practices that are concrete and real and making some impact, even though it's always against the odds, it's always a David vs. Goliath situation.

BB: When I hear you say "prophetic energies," I sense a notion of religion that amounts to "spirit," a religion that is spirit without content, with no theology, let's say.

CW: If we define culture—and here I think of Peter Burke's work, especially his book on the Italian Renaissance—if we define culture as values and attitudes that are embodied or expressed in texts, artifacts, or performances, sustained by communities over time, preserving various identities of unique individuals within those communities, then my understanding of religion, in particular Afro-American religion, would argue that within those embodiments and expressions there are, potentially, sources for egalitarian and democratic critiques of the powers that be. Now, the fact that those potential elements are realized only in very unique, very distinctive circumstances, makes them a prophetic tradition, always a marginal tradition, always a tradition of a small number of persons. This may seem like spirit without substantive content, because the substantive content of all religious traditions that we know are deeply conservative. But there are elements within that substantive content that lead some to move in prophetic directions, you see, though the dominant forms of religion are all deeply conservative, oftentimes quite repressive and reactionary, patriarchal, homophobic. A prophetic tradition I've always understood to be a very marginal tradition that's linked to certain kinds of energies that could be enacted in relation to different kinds of content that would borrow certain themes and motifs from religious traditions, but would couch them in narratives that tend to hit up against the dominant narratives within dominant religious traditions. This is what gets me into deep trouble. Surely, the elites within my own church, and the religious elites around the country, see me as someone simply wedded to modern notions of democracy and freedom, who then tries to appropriate certain themes and motifs from religious narratives that conform to modern notions of democracy and freedom. And to a certain degree, I'm guilty of that. It's just that I recognize that the preservation of communities and identities will always be a tainted affair. And

by "tainted," I mean you're going to have these conservative and reactionary elements within a religious tradition
that also preserves the very identities and communities
which are requisite for any kind of serious democratic
politics.

BB: This would be for you, then, a corrective to a
Marxist tradition that can't quite imagine such communities, such identities.

CW: Yes. It's crucial, of course, to accent the
strengths and insights the Marxist tradition provides as
well as to accent the blindnesses and silences. For me, the
Marxist tradition at its best is an instance of the longer
radical democratic tradition of the human adventure,
going back to Pericles' funeral oration and before, focusing
on citizens participating and expanding their sense of who
they are as individuals and as members of a community.
What Marx, what the Marxist tradition, tries to do is keep
track of those impediments within the economic sphere
that preclude democratization, that preclude workers participating in decisions that fundamentally affect their
lives, and that result in maldistribution of resources. The
Marxist tradition is a crucial moment, though flawed, in
trying to keep alive a radical democratic tradition in
which people participate in the decision-making processes
in those institutions that fundamentally regulate their
lives. The other great strength of the Marxist tradition is
that it always calls for connections to be made across
national, racial, and regional lines. It has an international
character, both in its analysis and in its project, that is
very important and of course overlaps with the Christianity that I promote—namely, it does believe that human
beings have a certain kind of dignity and value independent of nation, race, sexual orientation and what-have-
you. Now, the Marxist tradition is an instance of the
greater Romantic movement in the early nineteenth century, with its emphasis on human powers and human
agency to create that future in which individuality can

flower and flourish. It's in Schiller's letters, it's in the early Marx, you find it in the best of the Romantics. In terms of talking about history, the Marxist tradition is the best expression of a Romantic tradition of human making and remaking.

That's the good stuff—an instance of the radical democratic tradition, and an instance of the Romantic tradition. Now, the silences and blindnesses of Marx are as follows: a relative inability to understand the complexity of culture—issues of identity and so forth. When women and gays and lesbians and people of color look to the Marxist tradition for subtle understandings of community and identity, they're not going to find it. And then there is Foucault's point, let's say, that the Marxist understanding of power tends to be so thoroughly focused on structural institutions, conditions linked to the economy, that it doesn't understand power tied to the microphysics of a society, to use Foucault's jargon, to the various ways in which not only identities are created and institutions in civil societies operate, but ways in which resistance is generated, based on cultural resources far outside of the work place.

There's a sense in which Marx is not in any way true to the very traditions that I'm ascribing to his project, which is the radical democratic project, the Romantic project, because both of those traditions are fundamentally concerned about the kinds of things that Foucault and Du Bois and de Beauvoir are concerned about, you see, which is democratic participation, which is the human making and remaking of themselves for their own individual flourishing and for communal flourishing.

BB: And the "scientific" Marx?

CW: The Marx who became obsessed with scientificity and the scientific status of his work brought in a certain kind of orthodoxy and dogmatism in his work. If it takes wanting to be scientific to sharpen your analysis, OK, but taking that motivation as seriously as Marx did can lead in positivistic directions, and positivism for me is not just an intellectually indefensible position, but an immoral position to the degree to which it eliminates the question of the crucial role of values as real things in the world that fundamentally affect how we understand the world. When William James says that your understanding of the nature of reality is part of your moral life, it's one of the great pragmatic maxims that I thoroughly accept; you could not find a more powerful critique of positivism than that. When Marxism moves in positivistic directions, it opens itself to elite manipulation, ideologies of experts, managerial ideology, all the things we know that have gone hand in hand with positivism in the modern world, be it under a communist regime in terms of bureaucratic manipulation of ordinary people, or be it under a capitalistic regime in which you have the imposition of the experts' perspectives on the lives of ordinary people, all in the name of reproducing the bureaucratic class, or reproducing the managerial class. Positivism is not just an intellectual plaything but a fundamental cultural phenomenon that one has to resist in the name of democracy. Dewey understood that.

BB: For you, pragmatism returns, repeatedly, to refine an issue, to refine your own analysis, to support a critique of the status quo and to prompt imaginative alternatives...

CW: Pragmatism is unique as a philosophical tradition in the modern world in its preoccupation or near obsession with the meaning and value of democracy, and this is manifested on a variety of different levels. In the realm of knowledge, it means a certain defense of *doxa* vis-à-vis *episteme*. Now *doxa* was always degraded, going back to the *Republic*, going back to the Platonic dialogues. Pragmatism comes along and says, in fact, the best knowledge that we have is going to be nothing but warranted opinion, which could be wrong in the future. You get an experimentalism motored by the human wheel, voluntarism. You get a democratic sensibility that radically calls

into question the kinds of quests for certainty characteristic of so much of the philosophical vision before pragmatism arrived on the scene. In the ethical realm, it means,
then, that facts and values are on a continuum rather than
separated by a thick line of demarcation, which means
that ethics becomes the fundamental basis for aesthetics,
logic, epistemology, politics, and so on. You begin with a
conception of the moral life, and the moral life for pragmatists is one which acknowledges a uniqueness of who
one is as an individual, and the way in which that uniqueness has been thoroughly shaped by the community and
tradition of which one is in part a product. The stamp you
leave on the world, the blow that you make for freedom,
for justice, for love or whatever, is going to be one that is
on a continuum with the blow that all other human beings
make, though it will be distinct and unique. There's a
stress on the common person and common morality not as
a static and stable process, but as a very complex process
that all people undergo; so that the ordinary and the
quotidian and the mass and the popular are not something
left over after you've done all the good highbrow stuff.

BB: This emphasis on the individual, on the moral
life, this seems to situate us in a pre-Foucaultian, pre-
Lacanian, pre-Derridian moment.

CW: I would argue that pragmatists—Deweyans
especially—talk about the moral life in a way that is
always already post-Lacanian, post-Derridian, post-
Foucaultian. And what I mean by that is that pragmatism
takes for granted the social construction of identities. It
takes for granted the degree to which the unconscious
works as a language in the sense that it is always already
part and parcel of who we are and in some way influencing
our conceptions of who we are and trying to repress
certain aspects of ourselves; it takes for granted notions
of ideology in which it's true that our conceptions of
ourselves and society are symbolic interactions between
what a tradition has bequeathed to us and what our

aspirations are, what our desires are, and so on. You read a text like *Human Nature and Character*, in '22, by Dewey, or any work by George Herbert Mead, and the starting point is the social construction of the person; the starting point is the ways in which communal networks are always already in place prior to our understanding of what we are, what we do, what we hope for, what we aspire to, what we desire and so on. In that sense, Deweyan discourse about moral life is radically historicized; it's linked to deeply psychological understandings of the biologistic and the social coming together in this human organism that is responding to circumstances and that is attempting to sustain some sense of meaning and purpose through that interaction, what Dewey later in his career called "transaction" (in some ways a much better word). I think it's wrong to think pragmatism presupposes some glib humanist notion of the subject that's prior to language or prior to textuality. I think that there are certainly textual evidences in Mead and Dewey especially, but in Peirce as well, to respond to those who think that somehow pragmatism is pre-Derridian.

BB: Finally, I'd like you to say more about "class" as a cultural analytic—not "class" as the way to identify a proletariat or the supposed New Class of the 80s, but that bureaucratic "class" you spoke of, or the "elite" intellectual class that attends conferences. How do institutional structures affect the debate over multiculturalism, a theatricalized debate at times...

CW: The debate is on a continuum with the presidential debate every four years: it lacks intellectual substance, it's theatrical, its language tends to be technocratic and bureaucratic in order to appease a consumer-oriented audience, to convince them they ought to have access to the goodies, the benefits. You see, in American society, as you know, universities have played a disproportionate role as a moment in upward social mobility, so that education has been viewed primarily as a ladder up. But in a business civilization, in a hotel civilization, the fundamental operations of the market sit at the very center of the civilization, and education tends to be viewed only in the crudest instrumentalist forms. Therefore, much of the debate tends to be a debate over who has access to social and economic benefits, with very little sense of the deeper intellectual issues, the issues we've been talking about. It's different in Europe, of course, even though Europe's more elitist, provides less access to education, and has a class structure that's more ossified. I don't want to paint the American educational system as simply negative across the board, but today it is very difficult for serious intellectuals—who want to dig deep beneath the bureaucratic veneer of discourse about goodies, slots, curriculum, representation and so on—to believe that our understanding of the past relates to the present. But that's what the vocation of intellectuals is all about, in part. Given that, then, how do you function? Well, as we know, presidential debates lack intellectual substance for the most part, but they're very important because they do affect who has access to power and what kind of life chances people have, especially working and poor people. The same is true when it comes to this debate about multiculturalism because it does affect the distribution of benefits, the life chances of working people and poor people, who are disproportionately people of color. If you're concerned about human beings, you have to intervene, trying on the one hand to preserve whatever intellectual integrity the debate has, and trying to bring to bear one's own democratic politics. When one's opponents make no attempt to have any sense of intellectual integrity, then they become ideologues, and it's a battle over benefits. Bennett and Cheney only want to trot Plato and Arnold out as mythic figures in order to justify their understanding of cultural citizenship. You have to function on the level that you see most of the bureaucrats' energies functioning. And it's also true for some of the multiculturalists, themselves professional managers trying to make their bid for power and legitimacy, feeling marginalized in an academy that has been deeply racist and patriarchal. The racism of the academy is undeniable. But promoting access to texts as a means of supporting middle-class black careers, brown careers, women's careers, is something that I'm suspicious of, even as I agree with many of their concerns. It's very difficult and delicate, this situating of oneself in this debate, and one has to proceed very carefully and analyze the different levels of discourse going on without being naive about either one of those dimensions. I hope that's clear.

Race, Class & Power
in Contemporary America

I want to say first that it seems to me that what underlies the fine paper Dr. Callahan just gave is what I call loosely "the problematic of order," the sense of anarchy, chaos and disorder encroaching upon us that puts me in mind of some of the towering cultural figures of the modern West (especially Edmund Burke and Matthew Arnold), in which they attempted to conceive of a notion of order in relation to tradition. Of course, for Burke it had to do with trying to defend the very subtle conception of a dynamic order linked to a tradition that changes slowly, incrementally, by means of organic reform. And Matthew Arnold, of course, the author of that famous text of 1869, *Culture and Anarchy*—where he links culture to the quest for perfection—was always attempting on the one hand to promote and encourage standards of excellence, while on the other hand, acknowledged that this quest is perennial. But he also links culture to safety because he finds that "barbarians" are always at the gate. It is quite explicit; in fact, he's explicit in a way that very few conservatives and liberals are regarding the link between the preservation of order and the deployment of repression.

If you recall the famous moment in his text where he throws those who threaten the order off the Tarpeian rock used by the Romans to cast off criminals, you see that the Tarpeian rock is a metaphor for state power.[1] What does that have to do with Dr. Callahan's presentation? I think it has much to do with his presentation because he is preoccupied with a common moral culture (which I read as a signifier of some need to provide moral justification for order). Inter-generational sex signifies anarchy, chaos, the *reductio ad absurdum* of certain kinds of vulgar moral pluralism.

Now, I suspect that no one here in this room would want to defend inter-generational sex.

But the point is that there are other signifiers that are much more infused politically. Twenty years ago inter-racial sex was viewed as immoral, and in certain parts of the country, as illegal. There are debates today about gay and lesbian sex. People appeal to their traditions, and there are honorable persons on both sides in terms of trying to tease out resources in their tradition to reflect on what is the moral status of gay and lesbian sex and so forth.

In part, then, what I see Dr. Callahan attempting to do is to build on the best of Burke and Arnold, attempting to provide his own conception of what a moral justification of order looks like. I should say that by invoking Burke and Arnold I in no way want to ideologically trump the conversation. Burke and Arnold are open to a variety of ideological interpretations and political appropriations. I think it is no accident that the best book written on Edmund Burke was written by the young John Morley, who was the progressive disciple of the later John Stuart Mill, and the founder of the *Fortnightly Review* in Victorian England.[2] Or, that the best book I know of ever written on Matthew Arnold was that of the young left liberal critic Lionel Trilling in 1939. So, don't think by invoking a Burke or an Arnold you are necessarily tilting toward the right as is often assumed to be the case. I take these two figures quite seriously, and most people know I am quite explicitly on the left and will remain there as long as my arguments convince me, which they do at the moment. But the challenge of Burke and Arnold, I think, is quite profound.

I want first to distinguish between three different levels that will help us situate Dr. Callahan's argument. The first level is the normative level, the second is the descriptive, and the third is the analytical. By the normative I am talking about ought claims, what ought to be the case. I am talking about what the grounds and bases of those ought claims are, and it is at the normative level that we see Dr.

Callahan making his very important distinctions, a kind of mapping of the normative terrain with moral maximalism, moral minimalism, and moral relativism and then his own Burkean and Arnoldian conception of equipoise. Now he doesn't tell us specifically which tradition he actually wants to defend. I'm sure if he had more time he would flesh this out. But there is certainly some tradition lurking in the background here for which he would provide a very subtle and refined interpretation that would justify the kind of order he endorses. He certainly tells us that it is not going to be moral maximalism. I think we would all agree. He says he thinks minimalism is not enough. I happen to be a defender of the kind of moral minimalism, or at least, a version of moral minimalism that he is rejecting, so we have a disagreement here. Where we do agree is that we both have libertarian impulses. So even his defense of moral equipoise includes a libertarian dimension. He wants to defend liberal notions of tolerance, civility, mediating conflict, as do I. But he wants a thicker conception of moral agreement in our society. I would like to see a thicker conception too, but my hunch is that any moves in that direction would have authoritarian implications; and so trying to walk the tightrope between commitments to libertarian values on the one hand and commitment to democratic values on the other always makes me suspicious of any species of moral equipoise that trashes moral maximalism, as if that were the only version of authoritarianism, but could quite easily, and surreptitiously tuck away, an authoritarian seed within the moral equipoise position. This is a query and a question I would pose to Dr. Callahan, even as he would condemn any authoritarianism on the surface. One has to raise the question of whether there are still authoritarian seeds lurking beneath his position of moral equipoise.

I do not want to remain solely on this normative level. The descriptive level, involving claims about what is the case, is something that he states very briefly. He tells us that minimalism seems to be very pervasive these days, and we are tilting toward relativism. It is a description, a kind of report of where we are, and I would actually go farther and say I think that relativism is much more pervasive than you would suspect. I agree with Alasdair MacIntyre and others in this regard. We live in an emotivist culture in which subjectivism of the most sophomoric type, relativism of the "anything goes" type is more and more pervasive. But, my concern is with the third level, which is the analytical level to give an account of what is the case and what the possibilities are for the normative projects to which we subscribe. It seems to me in talking about power, be it moral power, which Dr. Callahan quite rightly acknowledges is his focus, it is ultimately inseparable from, although not reducible to, political power, to economic power, and to cultural power. Therefore, you have to talk about analysis, you have to talk about subtle social analysis, you also have to then couch it within a larger historical narrative. I must say, one of the more disappointing features of our time, and I do not say this as a critique of Dr. Callahan's paper—he had only 22 pages, and he can't do everything in 22 pages—but, it seems to me one of the most disappointing features, one of the most disempowering aspects of our moment in history is the lack of historical sense: the refusal to engage in a situating of ourselves in relation to larger historical narratives. There is a whole host of reasons for why that is so—which I don't have time to go into now. But, there is a turn away from history, either in a textualist form, or in a personalist form, or in a traditional form, in a dogmatic and orthodox manner, that also tries to hold the crucial role played by historical narratives at bay.

What I will attempt to do very briefly is to provide a sketch of what a social and analytical reading of our present moment is and its link to a larger historical narrative that forces us to talk about moral power in relation to political, economic, and cultural power. One begins, I think, by looking at our present moment. It is a moment, I want to argue, of relative economic decline, having to do with not simply unprecedented public and private debt, or short-term profiteering or an inadequate system of technical education for workers, but most importantly, the stubborn incapacity to mobilize resources in the public sphere, a public sphere that is hollow. This makes it very difficult for any kind of serious critical exchange to take place.

What we need are more public spheres in which serious critical exchange takes place, in which arguments bounce up against each other as arguments and not as *ad hominem* name-calling and finger-pointing. This has much to do with the undeniable cultural decay which is fundamentally the fact that people are losing trust in public institutions. This generates distrust of each other which makes argument nearly impossible and rational exchange difficult.

This undeniable cultural decay, I think, has to do fundamentally with the erosion of civil society: the shattered families, schools, and civic associations. Most importantly, I think, it has to do with the social breakdown in systems for nurturing children. I think that is a benchmark of an empire in decline, of a society in decay. The inability to transmit the purpose and meaning, excellence and elegance, dignity and decency to children; producing deracinated and denuded individuals with no sense of roots, with no cultural armor to navigate through the traumas and terrors of life—of death, disease, disappointment, and despair—we find ourselves caught up more and more within a market culture that provides us not with the "values" but with hedonistic self-indulgence, and upward mobility. This weakens our ability to take non-market values seriously, like love and commitment and justice and solidarity and community. Powerful market forces provide a market morality, market religion, and market politics that have become pervasive in American society. And, as you can imagine, one could write a book on each one of these subjects.

But I touch on it just very briefly because even Adam Smith recognized that one had to read *The Theory of Moral Sentiments* along with *The Wealth of Nations* to get an idea of what he understood the good society to be. He never conceived of a market culture providing any justification for markets in the economy. I think most of us recognize markets in the economy are inescapable and indispensable for preservation of liberties, but they are necessary and not sufficient conditions for the good society. When a market culture fundamentally shapes our conception of ourselves, our children's conception of themselves and each other, they produce a cold-hearted and mean-spirited disposition toward the world. I think it has something to do in a highly complex way with the escalation of violence of our social fabric, which justifies our concern with order. I think almost every American I know is concerned with order, in part because of the escalation of the violence in our social fabric—especially the violence against women. I think it has much to do with the Thomas hearings, actually, but also with violence against gays and lesbians and the general xenophobic violence we see as a whole. Now, if these very cryptic remarks have anything to do with where we are, then the question becomes: how do we find ourselves in this particular situation?

I suggested last night that we have to begin with the fact that we have experienced something unprecedented in our history as a nation, which is the massive redistribution of wealth and income from working people and lower-middle-class people to the upper-middle-class and the well-to-do. It does not explain everything, but it is one starting point. Withdrawal of resources from a group of people who are already experiencing downward mobility, given the end of the American century, which was 1973 (it began in 1945) and the redistribution of their wealth and especially their income, going hand in hand with the escalating cultural decay, is a lethal linkage that produces tribal frenzy and xenophobic strife. This is one dimension of our time. If it continues, I think most of us recognize, we will enter a long and dark tunnel of increasing disorder, cultural anarchy, and communal chaos.

It is not simply the massive redistribution from the bottom up that I am talking about. It also has to do with the realignment of political forces that in part justified this redistribution. I think, here in American culture, the issue of race becomes fundamental. In 1964 the GOP Republicans supported the Civil Rights Bill and Voting Rights Bill far beyond the Democrats. In 1964 most black voters could not decide which party to support. It is very interesting in this regard.

I may not have time, but just think about this. In 1964 the Civil Rights Bill—the House GOP was 80 percent in favor.[3] In the Senate—the Democrats voted 66 to 34 and the Republicans voted 82 to 18.[4] Of course, we know why: Southern Democrats. But the point is that we had not yet so thoroughly racialized the political alignment at that time. Something happened between 1965 and 1968 and Richard Nixon understood this well. Of course, we know the story of Mr. Harry Dent, who had played such a fundamental role as principal advisor for Strom Thurmond, who walked out of the Democratic Party in 1948 to form the Dixiecrats. (It's ironic to see now the black women who were applauding Thurmond yesterday as he supported Clarence Thomas. America is a very strange land: not that they are *a priori* wrong or right. They have arguments, and we have to hear those arguments.)

But the fact is that the same Harry Dent, who was the architect behind the Dixiecrats, would play a role as well in what George Wallace tried to do in 1968: appealing to white, ethnic, working-class voters, and using race as a way of polarizing and dividing the electorate. He would serve as the principal architect for Nixon's "Southern strategy" of 1968. (Kevin Phillips would write about that a year later, as a conservative, just as he writes now as a populist, upset with the realignment he promoted.) It is very interesting when one reads in 1970 that Mr. Spiro Agnew says that his explicit strategy, using his own words, "was to create a positive polarization in America." He goes on, "dividing the American people has been my main contribution to the national political scene. I not only plead guilty to this charge, but I am somewhat flattered by it."[5] This is Mr. Agnew is 1970. Why? Because he recognized that the re-alignment of political forces would, in fact, deploy race especially as a way of undergirding a GOP strategy for the White House, for presidential power.

Now our younger people, who are preoccupied not so much with inter-generational sex, but who have been shaped by this moment, beginning in 1968, grew up in an atmosphere of escalating xenophobic attitudes and actions. There is very little sense of other options on the political scene, very little sense of countervailing forces which could be used to bring critique to bear on it. In a period of economic contraction, such as the recession of 1982, and of course, the recession of our present moment, to talk about economic, political, and cultural power means, at least, to acknowledge the role that these particular forces play. And we can debate about it. One doesn't have the time to lay out a detailed argument, but we must have a debate about it and talk about power and why we seem to put ourselves in a corner, as it were. I must submit that it is not simply a matter of talking about economics, politics, and cultural decay, but also the very deep existential implications as well. And what I mean by that is, the sense that as modern human beings cast in a Newtonian universe, viewing ourselves as bodies in space, no longer linked to a cosmic order, there is always the quest not only for meaning, but also a quest for belonging and community as well.

The kind of belonging and community that has served as the most attractive way of providing human beings with some sense of who they are and sustaining their existence as they meet inevitable and unavoidable extinction has been nation and race in the modern period; it also has been gender, and for a few in the world, it is profession. What this means is that the very notion of ideologies that high-light the universalism and internationalism has declined.

Even efforts for transcommunal interaction are weakening. It is hard to imagine how, in fact, they can be regenerated. This is something we are going to work on. I would argue that religious resources in the modern world are probably the most powerful for generating universalist views of the world. But we all know the dominant forms of our religious institutions are as caught within the xenophobia and the tribal frenzy as any other institutions.

Yet we do have some resources for regeneration. Marxism was once an attempt to provide a universal and international project that was traduced by a certain kind of nationalism and repressive elite in Russia. The Enlightenment was once such an effort, but it was traduced by white supremacist and male supremacist efforts. I think, in many ways, in 1945 the concentration camps were really the end of the international potential of the modern European *Aufklärung*. But where do you go? The Lombard League in Italy flourishes, as does LePen in France. You read about the attacks on Gypsies and foreigners just this past weekend in Germany and Czechoslovakia, all flourishing. Skinheads are flourishing. Quest for meaning now often takes xenophobic forms. What resources in our traditions enable us to go beyond this? I think ultimately it is going to be a question of the crisis in leadership in talking about moral power. This challenge of visionary leadership is fundamental if we are to overcome the present crisis.

I want to highlight four major moments in the kind of leadership I am suggesting. The first is that of human discernment. By human discernment I mean a broad and deep analytical grasp of the present in light of the past. The second moment is that of human connection, which in many ways, is the most important. How, in fact, do we go about engaging in a sincere and sacrificial effort to keep track of and never lose sight of the humanity of persons? This means we must reject Manichean perspectives—which means neither demonizing nor deifying those in power or those who are powerless. The third moment is that of human hypocrisy, which is exercising bold and defiant political courage to point out the discrepancy between principles and practices, between words and deeds. And last is that of human hope—an audacious attempt to inspire and energize world-weary people of good will. How do we convince them—how do we convince ourselves—that the future is indeed open-ended, that history is indeed unfinished, that the world is incomplete, that what we think and what we do does make a difference? This is something that all of us have to grapple with—a kind of skeleton hanging in our closet.

The ultimate aim of visionary leadership is to speak to our needs and wants by appealing to the better angels of our natures, as Lincoln put it. It is to lay bare the best of our potential, push us to the limits of this potential and exemplify these limits in attitude and in action.

The first moment of human discernment for the makings of visionary leaders seems to me to have to go hand in hand with at least a perception of economic decline and cultural decay, and again, economic decline and cultural decay is the challenge, it is not the conclusion. It is where we are. It in no way means that we must arrive there, only that there are, in fact, new possibilities.

How can it take place, how do you keep track of the humanity and create the requisite coalitions and alliances, not simply to bring political power and pressure to bear, but also to re-shape the atmosphere of the nation. William James wrote an essay on the occasion of the invasion, the occupation and the annexation of the Philippines by the United States in the latter part of the 19th century. William James was vice president of the Anti-Imperialist League in the early part of the 20th century and he wrote a fascinating essay called, "On a Certain Blindness in Human Beings." What he was struggling with was why the American press had so thoroughly demonized the Philippines as if they were some picture to be drawn rather than human beings to sympathize with. How did they lose contact with the humanity of the Filipino in this imperial drive? And what James suggested was that human beings have a tremendous difficulty in walking in other people's shoes and in trying to get in other people's skins and putting themselves in other person's situations. It doesn't necessarily mean that you agree with the person, but you engage in an act of what the great German philosopher, Wilhelm Dilthey called "empathetic understanding," which meant that even in dialogue with others, there was a human connection that allowed you to understand what kinds of fears and paranoia and anxiety they were going through. Even if intellectually you disagreed with their position, there was still a humanizing experience that also acknowledged, quite candidly, the disagreement and the conflict.

Now, I don't want to equalize the suffering of all of us, nor do I want to excuse talking about taking a stand. Our suffering is not the same in terms of socially induced suffering. It's very different from what we've been reading in the *New York Times* about the Harlem families, who those of us who spend time there recognize quite readily. But the human connection can be made in light of the degree to which the power differential is acknowledged. This is what it seems to me we're losing—a visionary leadership has to keep track of this, or there will be no cultural resources to talk about progressive politics, no sense of hope to talk about possible coalition and alliances, it seems to me. Now, I think that one example is manifest in our public language and our public rhetoric and our public discourse. The very categories and concepts that we use tend to reinforce the polarization that we claim to be against, and therefore, little sense of complexity, subtlety, ambiguity and equivocality surfaces, and it precludes decent and candid communication in public opinion. Nowhere is this more apparent, it seems to me, than the cluster of issues related to race and class as manifest in a debate between so-called Eurocentrists and Multi-culturalists. Of course, this is a debate that is raging now. The next thing you know, those who talk about race and gender and class become the few fascists of the Left. When we use that word, Fascist, it makes me shake; I think of Hitler, Mussolini. Then I turn to my friends, I say, you: Mussolini, Hitler? What kind of language is this? Inflation of rhetoric. Then, of course, in many ways the Left is responsible for an inflation of rhetoric as well, but it reflects the polarization that we're talking about here.

I want to make a few points about this because it seems to me we have to come up with—not simply taking the right position, but also trying to cast the debate in such a way that the polarization does not preclude any possibility of transforming the situation in which we find ourselves.

First, I want to suggest that the terms themselves, Eurocentrism and Multi-culturalism, are bureaucratic categories rather than substantive intellectual positions. What I mean by this is there's a certain way of packaging a debate, giving it a certain theatricality for sensationalist purposes, and it means then that we're never able to acknowledge dynamic changing, revisable historical legacies that themselves are always ambiguous, always carry certain insights and blindnesses, always have something good and bad, something positive and negative. The Age of Europe certainly has much to teach humankind, just as those hegemonic empires before the Age of Europe. But the question is, how do we tease out of these grand contributions and achievements the best of us human creatures? It's not just a matter of the greatness of Shakespeare or of Toni Morrison. That's for bureaucrats to decide. Toni Morrison is as profound in her way as William Shakespeare is profound in his way. All you have to do is read them. The point is, how, in fact, do we tease out what Shakespeare was getting at? There are so many different ways. And what Toni Morrison is getting at in so many different ways. A subtle articulation of what it means to be human, both in their rendition of the human condition, as well as the values that could come forth upon which we can build our political struggles.

That's the real challenge, it seems to me, and this is the first step toward thinking historically and keeping track of persons' humanity, all, of course, persons born in circumstances not of their own choosing. But even a more dangerous issue here is that the debate itself rarely raises the issues of how any text or any paintings or any buildings are to be interpreted. You can read Alice Walker in a flat-footed sophomoric way; you can read Chekhov in a flat-footed sophomoric way; and you still miss what's there. The question is how do you approach these texts? How do any of these texts stay vital and vibrant? What happens when you have a bureaucratic debate and a whole generation that doesn't give a damn about Toni Morrison, Shakespeare, Chekhov, Tolstoy or anybody else?

In other words, there's a much larger, deeper intellectual agenda at work for those who are concerned with the common good and active citizenry. That's my point. Issues such as the quality of argument, the accuracy of historical rendering, the integrity of educating an active citizenry for the 21st century tend to be reduced to mere one-upmanship or manipulation on the one hand, or just the defense of entrenched groups and self-interest on the other. Again, it's sensationalizing for private ends rather than the much needed critical exchange for the public good. And last, in relation to this debate, it tends to downplay the hybrid character of any culture— by hybrid I mean the degree to which any culture is shot through with a variety of different sources, antecedent cultural fragments being deployed in new ways to produce something novel. This is the only way in which a culture survives and thrives and once the hybrid character of any culture is acknowledged, it means that we also have looked at the degree to which every culture and nation has been in some way linked to some form of barbarism. In this way, ahistorical and Manichean ways of thinking, not only polarize, but also hold at arm's length, a common humanity and different social positions and different cultural positions. Civic virtue and public responsibility have as much to do with the categories we use as with the deeds we perform.

The third moment is that of human hypocrisy and I want to invoke the epigram from one of the leading young New York intellectuals at the turn of the century. His name is Randolph Bourne. He died at the young age of 32 years old in December of 1918. He had a misshapen dwarf's body and a twisted face. He's one of the towering public intellectual figures between 1907 and 1918. He wrote a famous essay called "The War and the Intellectuals"—again, worth re-reading especially in these times—and he says, "Idealism should be kept for what is ideal." Think about that. Idealism should be kept for what is ideal! It seems to me that what Randolph Bourne is getting at in relation to this third moment of human hypocrisy is that idealism is not boosterism, just as critique is not castigation. But idealism is a bold and defiant highlighting of hypocrisy in that this highlighting of hypocrisy is the go-cart for constitutional and democratic processes. It is a self-critical and self-correcting procedure. Hypocrisy can be found in high places of the powerful as well as in places of the powerless. Lord Acton was only partly right—that absolute power does indeed corrupt absolutely; the lack of power also corrupts. It cuts both ways. I think this is precisely what Malcolm X had in mind when he provided his technical definition of what a nigger was. Do you recall what he said? He said, "a nigger is a victim of American democracy." And note the oxymoronic character and self-contradictory character of this formulation. How could there be a victim of American democracy? Because you point out the hypocrisy and how hypocrisy becomes institutionalized and legalized and you end up with a kind of *herrenfolk* democracy which, of course, in many ways was the case in the USA until the 1950s. But the very processes of democratic change and democratization had been hemorrhaged and blocked, and yet only better constitutional and better democratic processes could ameliorate it.

The escalation and inflation of hypocrisy encourages

wholesale opportunism and it raises, it seems to me, some of the most terrifying questions that we have when we talk about issues of race, gender and class. Namely, are we foolish to look at society and the world through moral microscopes, with egalitarian sentiments and libertarian sensibilities and think that unnecessary and alterable human suffering can be lessened? Can, and does, this kind of social hope have a role and place in our world? And keep in mind, we are living in a particular moment in our culture in which the larger systems of thought and systems of belief tend to be collapsing around us. It's not just communism and the dissolution of the Soviet empire, it's not just liberal legalism that tends more and more to be unable to deal with the cultural issues as well as the political ones, it is not just, of course, the religious world views that themselves are so thoroughly intertwined with the kind of cultural decay and decline that I've mentioned. At this particular moment in the 20th century, we hope that fear and loathing and hatred have not put our dreams of freedom and democracy to sleep, as it were. And this is why the issues of human hope become fundamental for any of those who have the audacity to be, or project, some model of visionary leadership in this particular moment.

Decline and decay are quite real, but doom and gloom are not the last words. We must give up all nostalgia for a golden age. What I mean by this is that any golden age, any stable moment of the past, was predicated on some people's pain and suffering, a pain and suffering that, no longer desirable, never was and certainly is no longer possible. Give up any beliefs, naive beliefs, about inevitable progress, but at the same time recognize progress is always possible though never ineluctable. Give up any notion that the saving power resides in our efficient toys and I think that's very important these days—the kind of military and technological triumphalism we see displayed on television. Give up any romanticizing and idealizing of the people but, by never losing contact with their humanity, acknowledging they have tremendous potential and tremendous possibility when in fact, their energies are galvanized in a moral manner and some sense of possibility and belief in themselves is reinforced. Visionary leadership, then, is predicated on a leap of faith and a labor of love. The Pascalian wager on the mental and moral capacities of common people, and a sacrificial example of a genuine love that exudes and encourages people's confidence in themselves and those who have the privilege to serve them as leaders. And without this, it seems to me, we can talk on and on about the statistics, on and on about how we try to mobilize resources, on and on about how greedy the rich are and how ungracious the poor seem to be, given all of the social programs, as the conservatives often put forth—the voices can go on and on in the Tower of Babel, but it will give us very little push toward where we must go. Because if not, it seems to me, we are on the road to self-destruction. Chaos, anarchy, disorder are already at work in a variety of different communities and spreading, which means then, that the democratic faith that Whitman put forth, we find in imperfect yet powerful ways. And Thomas Jefferson—slaveholder, yes—democratic theorist, yes—dialectical reading needed. There's no way of understanding modern democracy without reading Thomas Jefferson and yet the hypocrisy must be pointed out—slaveholder, yes. That's the kind of subtle reading necessary. Ralph Waldo Emerson, another grand figure within this democratic parade; Frederick Douglass, Abraham Lincoln, Sojourner Truth, Chief Joseph of the Nez Perce, immortalized by Robert Penn Warren's powerful poem of the 70s, Mother Jones, Michael Harrington, Harvey Milk, Abraham Joshua Heschel, Martin Luther King, Jr., and thousands of other anonymous visionary leaders on the local level. And I have to say this because in a televisual culture there's a notion that you're not a leader unless you're on television, which reinforces the dominant personality of our time, which is the addictive personality. You become addicted to the cameras, just as most of us are addicted to

some form of stimulation in order to sustain some vitality
and vibrancy of the self, rendering us spectatorally passive,
engaging in forms of therapeutic release in order to sense
that we are still alive. But this democratic parade who lit
flickering candles of hope in difficult and troubled times is,
it seems to me, that cloud of witnesses to whom we must
look.

There is a great American songwriter who died last
year. His name is James Cleveland. He wrote some marvel-
ous songs, but there is one song I think most of you know, it
was the song sung immediately after Jesse Jackson's historic
presidential address in San Francisco in 1984, and the song
was entitled "Ordinary People." Do you remember that
song? It was a powerful song, not just the form, not just the
style, but the words, the lyrics. Because what James Cleveland was able to do, as an artistic creator of the black church
tradition that helped shape him, was to link human possibility, ordinary people's capacity and that even when it
looked as if ordinary people can only do a little, that little
makes a lot of difference. It becomes much, as he puts it,
when within the body politic there's visionary leadership
that can tease out the confidence, the affirmation, the notion
that we can make a difference when, indeed, our common
humanity is affirmed, given our differences. We're not elid-
ing and erasing the differences, we're acknowledging differences that affirm a connection, overlap. And it seems to
me that James Cleveland, like the great and late Frank
Capra, is expressing something very deep within American
culture. And once we lose that notion, then it seems to me
that we begin to lose all.

There's a very famous letter that Horace Walpole
wrote to Horace Mann in the eighteenth century where he
said, "You know, I've often thought that the world is a
comedy to those who think and a tragedy to those who feel,
which helps explain to me why Democratus laughed and
Heraclitus wept." And it seems to me we cannot but think
and feel, laugh and weep, but, with the belief and capacity

of ordinary people we can also fight. With a smile on our faces, tears in our eyes, we see the deprivation, we hold up a bloodstained banner in which some sense of hope based on discernment and connection, pointing out hypocrisy, keeping alive some sense of possibility, can be projected both for ourselves, for our children and for our sacred honor.

Identity:
A Matter of Life and Death

I'd first like to congratulate those who had the vision and determination to bring us together, for one can see that this is quite a relevant and pertinent issue. And I'm sure that the organizers did not know that the conference would be held the same day that David Duke was up for election in the state where my mother and father were born—old Jim and Jane Crow Louisiana. Nor did they know that it would be the day after Michael Jackson decided to make his statement about identity—black or white—in a video. But I think this matter raises three fundamental questions that I want to zoom in on very quickly. The first is "What do we mean by *'identity'*?" Since this term itself can be a rather elusive, amorphous, and even vaporous one, we need to have heuristic markings for it. The second is "What is the moral content of one's identities?"—because we all have multiple positions in terms of constructing our identities; there's no such thing as having one identity or of there being one essential identity that fundamentally defines who we actually are. And third, "What are the political consequences of our various identities?"—which is what Joan Scott was talking about with such insight.

So let's begin with a heuristic definition. For me identity is fundamentally about desire and death. How you construct your identity is predicated on how you construct desire and how you conceive of death: desire for recognition; quest for visibility (James Baldwin—*No Name in the Street; Nobody Knows my Name*); the sense of being acknowledged; a deep desire for association—what Edward Said would call affiliation. It's the longing to belong, a deep, visceral need that most linguistically conscious animals who transact with an environment (that's us) participate in.

And then there is a profound desire for protection, for security, for safety, for surety. And so in talking about identity we have to begin to look at the various ways in which human beings have constructed their desire for recognition, association, and protection over time and in space and always under circumstances not of their own choosing.

But identity also has to do with death. We can't talk about identity without talking about death. That's what a brother named Julio Rivera had to come to terms with: the fact that his identity had been constructed in such a way that xenophobes would put him to death. Or brother Youssef Hawkins in Bensonhurst. Or brother Yankel Rosenbaum in Crown Heights. Persons who construct their identities and desires often do it in such a way that they're willing to die for it—soldiers in the Middle East, for example—or, under a national identity, that they're willing to kill others. And the rampant sexual violence in the lives of millions of women who are attacked by men caught up in vicious patriarchal identities—this speaks to what we're talking about. But if in fact identity has something to do with these various kinds of desires, these various conceptions of death (we are beings-toward-death), it's because we have, given our inevitable extinction, to come up with a way of endowing ourselves with significance.

So we weave webs of existential meaning. We say something about the terrors of nature, the cruelties of fate, the unjustified suffering. It sounds very much like religion. But let's understand: religion not in the theological sense, but in the etymological sense of *ligare*, which means to bind. Identity is about binding, and it means, on the one hand, that you can be bound—parochialist, narrow, xenophobic. But it also means that you can be held together in the face of the terrors of nature, the cruelties of fate, and the need for some compensation for unjustified suffering: what theologians used to call the problem of evil. And believe me, identity cuts at that deep existential level where religion resides. That's what's frightening, especially for the left that, like Habermas, has linked itself to an Enlightenment bandwagon. For it's a shaking of the rationalist foundation.

But keep in mind, here, the crucial interplay between desire and death, the quest for existential meaning and material resources. For identity is about bodies, land, labor, and instruments of production. It's about the distribution of resources. That's, in part, what David Duke is all about. He's addressing a background condition of the maldistribution of resources in which downward mobility is forcing a working class, squeezed by taxes and exploited by a ruling group, to race-bait and scapegoat black folk, Jewish people, and women. So we must always keep in mind the role of material resources and the various systems that generate their distribution and consumption. There has to be a dialectical interplay in talking about these things; and of course that's one of the problems of a narrow and xenophobic identity politics or political positions. Such positions cause us to lose sight of the fact that we linguistically conscious animals have, up to this moment, had to labor under a radically inegalitarian distribution of resources.

And we thus come to our second question: "What is the moral content of your identity?" It's another way of raising the question of how radically democratic are you when you talk about defining your identity, especially in relation to this maldistribution of resources. If this is important, it's because one of the most disturbing things about identity talk—especially in America, but my hunch is it's true around the world—is that when people speak about identity, they always begin by talking about the victims. Having a conference on race? Bring on the black folk. We don't want to invite some white racists so they can lay bare the internal dynamics of what it is to be a white racist. No. Having a conference on gender? Bring on women. As if whiteness is not as fundamentally constructed within the discourse of race as blackness is. As if maleness is not as fundamentally structured in the discourse of gender as is femaleness, or woman. As if straightness were inscribed into the nature of things, and those who are not straight have to provide some account of their identity. No, let's talk about identity-from-above as well as identity-from-below. That's something that is rarely stressed, rarely examined, rarely specified. We need to get a handle on how this whiteness, maleness, and straightness functions over time and space in relation to blackness or brownness or yellowness or womanness or gayness or lesbianness, etc.

I would hope that in our studies as well as in our discussions we recognize the very different status—the different political status—between identity from above and from below. I think this has much to do with the degree to which, when we talk about identities, we rarely speak of some of the larger identities that shape up. For example, national identity—which is very different from having a nation-state—is one of the most powerful means of constructing desire and death in our present moment. It functions on a different axis from that of race or gender, but with dialectic affinities. Why? Because there are racialized subjects who are deeply linked to national identity. That's one of the fascinating things about black neo-conservatives: they're against identity (they're thinking about black identity), but they are also the most rampant American nationalists in the country. The same thing would be true on other axes as well.

Thus addressing the moral content of one's identity forces us to raise the question of what and where the radical democratic project is. To what degree is that project called into question by certain narrow forms of identity politics? And what social basis could there be for a radical democratic project? I'm not going to answer that, but I'm raising the question. I think this is something that we have to grapple and come to terms with.

But I want to end by saying something about the last question, the one about the political consequences of one's identities. Since this has to do with strategies and tactics, it is something the left rarely talks about. Intellectuals usually have little to say about this. How do you go about binding people? What is the political version of the *ligare* activity, which is to say, mobilizing and organizing? Although at this present moment, one cannot, must not, give up on the radical democratic project, yet we find ourselves up against a wall in trying to put forward effective ways of mobilizing and organizing.

Yes, the left is balkanized; yes, the left is fragmented. The older universalist projects of the left have been shattered—shattered in part because they did not speak effectively to desire and death: they are an Enlightenment project whose critical acumen we must preserve but whose glib pseudo-universalisms we must radically call into question. As long as we simply hide various particularisms, but without that critical acumen, there cannot be a radical democratic project. So there must be strategies and tactics that cut across identity politics, cut across region, and gender, race, and class. Class is still around even though it's been unable to constitute an identity that has the saliency and potency of the other identities. And we must attempt to think about how we create and sustain organizations that acknowledge this. Because we're in the bind we're in partly because we've been unable to generate the transgendered, transracial, transsexual orientation of social motion, social momentum, social movement. And if we can't do that, then there will be many, many more David Dukes by the end of the twentieth century, even while we engage in our chatter about identity.

So we have a crucial organizational, strategic, and tactical imperative. It's not that we have to have an organizational meeting, but we have to engage the question of mobilization as an object of reflection, because as Joan Scott said, politics and thinking go hand in hand. And while our politics are understood in a multi-dimensional and multi-layered way it is also true that, on the ground, without the kind of social motion, momentum and movement that I'm talking about, we'll feel ourselves more and more pushed against the wall as the xenophobes—be it the Lombard League in Italy, or the skinheads in Germany, or Le Pen in France—more and more speak their right-wing constructs of desire and death to mobilize and organize *their* populace.

And that's serious business. When you get working-class folk, lower middle-class folk in Louisiana saying that what they see reminds them of Germany in 1930, that's not a plaything. And of course black folk know that by experience. That is a serious challenge.

Black Radicalism
and the Marxist Tradition

Cedric Robinson's *Black Marxism: The Making of the Black Radical Tradition* (London: Zed Press, 1983) is the most significant challenge to American Marxist and black left thought and practice since Harold Cruse's *The Crisis of the Negro Intellectual* (1967). Unfortunately, Robinson's book has not yet received the kind of critical attention it deserves. Though published in 1983, the book has already fallen through the cracks—a fate to be avoided if at all possible. This negligence results from the rather disjointed state of the American academic Left and the dismal state of the black intellectual Left: the former has become virtually captive to jargon-ridden discourses in which race receives little or no attention, and the latter is thoroughly disorganized, with no visible means of cultivating and sustaining high-level critical exchange.

Robinson's book is a towering achievement. There is simply nothing like it in the history of black radical thought. It is, in many ways, too ambitious. Yet in trying to do too much, Robinson raises the most fundamental questions facing both the black and white Left in America: to what extent are Marxist explanations of social history capable of grasping the many dimensions of racial oppression? What is and ought to be the relation of black resistance to broader working class insurgency? What is distinctive about dominant forms of black radicalism in contrast to non-black forms? How ought black left intellectuals to relate to the Marxist tradition?

Though more international in scope and erudite in execution, Robinson's project is similar to Cruse's in that it challenges black intellectuals to reconsider Afro-American thought and practice in light of the specificity of the black radical tradition. Like Cruse, Robinson believes that left black intellectuals tend uncritically to accept Marxist analyses which force them "to surrender the cultural survival of their people, the emergent revolutionary consciousness of black nationalism." (p. 435) Unlike Cruse, Robinson does not reject Marxist analyses but wants to use a Marxist *method* in order to discredit Eurocentric practitioners of Marxism. He concurs that a conception of the forces and relations of production is basic to the critique of capitalist societies—but he also accentuates the importance of cultural terrains of ideological struggle, such as affirming African identities in the face of negative images of blackness in the modern West.

Robinson's fundamental aim is to show that efforts to understand black peoples' history of resistance through the exclusive prism of Marxist analysis are incomplete and inaccurate. This is so because Marxist analyses tend to presuppose European models of history and experience—models that downplay the significance of black people as agents and black communities as conduits of cultural and political resistance. Robinson shows how the conditions of the emergence of Marxism in nineteenth-century Europe affected its formulations of class analysis and revolutionary struggle, illustrates how classic Marxist histories have ignored the role of race in the class formation of modern societies, discusses the content and character of the black radicalism overlooked by most Marxist thinkers, and reveals the ways in which major black intellectuals such as W.E.B. Du Bois, C.L.R. James, and Richard Wright tried to make Marxist theory more attuned to the black condition in the modern world.

Like that of most contemporary social scientists, Robinson's writing style is a bit off-putting. Yet the fascinating accounts that move his argument along make it well worth the effort. The scope of his scholarship is impressive; the force of his formulations, often persuasive. He takes the reader by the hand and walks him or her through the complex workings of the modern world, emphasizing the way in which capitalist modes of production shaped and were shaped by clashing ethnic, national, and racial allegiances. He then puts forward a critical re-reading of E.P. Thompson's classic *The Making of the English Working Class*, in light of Thompson's glaring omission of racialism. Robinson's criticism is not that Thompson should simply have added a few remarks about non-British workers to his account of British working class formation, but rather that to take race seriously he would have had to link the formation of British working class consciousness to Anglo-Saxon chauvinism, Irish anti-colonial rebellions (like that of 1798), and the trans-Atlantic African slave trade. Robinson concludes that though working class radicalism is a significant form of resistance to Western capitalism, it is often supportive of certain other defining features of Western civilization such as racialism and chauvinism. In this sense—at the economic, political, and cultural levels—"the European proletariat and its social allies did not constitute *the* revolutionary subject of history, nor was working class consciousness necessarily *the* negation of bourgeois culture." (pp. 4-5)

After this examination of the origins and limitations of European working class radicalism, Robinson turns to the roots of black radicalism. His basic thesis is that while black radicalism in the New World is situated and located within Western capitalist societies, it cannot be fully understood in light of Western models of radicalism. For Robinson, black radicalism

> is not a variant of Western radicalism whose proponents happen to be black. Rather, it is a specifically African response to an oppression emergent from the immediate determinants of European development in the modern era and framed by orders of human exploitation woven into the interstices of European social life from the inception of Western civilization. (p. 97)

The distinctive features of black radicalism, in other

words, must be linked to the traditions of Africa and black people's unique status of being degraded and despised human beings in a racist modern Western civilization. African traditions—religions, customs, folklore, mores—serve as crucial sources for collective resistance against economic exploitation, political oppression, *and* cultural degradation, as Robinson illustrates through detailed examinations of events ranging from the great Palmares settlement in Brazil (1605-1695) to the Haitian revolution (1804).

Robinson is right to accentuate the non-European sources of black resistance—as have progressive anthropologists like St. Clair Drake and Michael Taussig. Yet Robinson fails to give historically specific and socially pertinent accounts of the precise nature of those sources. Instead, he throws out phrases like "the preservation of the ontological totality granted by a metaphysical system which had never allowed for property" (p. 243) or "a shared philosophy developed in the African past and transmitted as culture." (p. 443) Such allusions to the cosmological and moral dimensions of African cultures are fine, yet they prove insufficient if we are to grasp the complex relations between communities, resistance, and commitment in the intersections between black and white peoples. Leonard Harris has made this point in his intriguing attempt to reformulate Robinson's talk about preserving the collective being or ontological totality into a conception of black nationalism as an African mode of collective being-in-the-world shaping and being shaped by prevailing capitalist processes.[1] The ultimate danger here is to fall prey to a romantic, idealized conception of a monolithic and homogeneous African past free of social contradictions, cultural blindnesses, and economic injustices. Robinson does not actually fall into this trap, but he comes close when he claims that indiscriminate violence and brutality "did not come naturally to African peoples" due to the resolution of conflict in Africa by means of migration and resettlement rather than by fratricidal warfare as in Europe. (p. 443)

The last section of Robinson's work, which composes almost half of the book, is the most controversial. It focuses on the black left intelligentsia. Robinson tries to show the continuities between "the black rebellions of the previous centuries and the first articulations of a world revolutionary theory in the present century" (p. 252) by examining the major works of three towering black intellectuals who struggled with Marxist theory: W.E.B. Du Bois, C.L.R. James, and Richard Wright. Robinson's treatment of each of these figures is problematic, not only because he fails to convey the complexity and richness of their thought, but also because they don't fit well into his project of upholding the radical depth and cultural density of revolutionary black nationalism. Du Bois, James, and Wright have little to say about this tradition, and what they do have to say is highly ambiguous and equivocal in relation to Robinson's project.

Robinson's readings of Du Bois, James, and Wright are always intriguing and informed. Yet they are neither persuasive nor convincing. Robinson's W.E.B. Du Bois—"one of the two most sophisticated Marxist theorists in America" (p. 266)—fails to ring true. Du Bois's links to the black revolutionary nationalist tradition were always tenuous, even as a Marxist influenced historian in the 1930s and thereafter. Robinson does not distinguish between Du Bois's appreciation of the black culture of resistance and his distance from a black nationalist perspective. So in his reading of Du Bois, Robinson must conclude that the black nationalist heritage appeared to Du Bois's "Westernized eyes [as] part legend, part whimsy, part art." (p. 324)

Robinson's C.L.R. James is a fascinating figure who goes beyond European radical thought in response to the 1934 Italian invasion of Ethiopia. "From this point on his work would lead beyond the doctrinaire constructions of the anti-Stalinist Left and Engels and Marx themselves. The force of the black radical tradition merged with the exigencies of black masses in movement to form a new theory and ideology in James' writings." (p. 382) But what was this new theory and ideology? From what Robinson says, it amounts to calls for self-determination by any means necessary. This is a courageous and convincing slogan, but it is neither a theory nor ideology. James remained, for the most part, a creative thinker within and a loyal member of the Trotskyist tradition with only *strategic* relations to the black revolutionary heritage Robinson highlights. Robinson ends his chapter on James with praise for James' thorough criticism of Western Marxism in his *Notes on Dialectics*, yet ignores James' own comment that he always remained a "black European" and "[his] whole life was toward European literature, European sociology." (quoted in Robinson, p. 396)

Lastly, Robinson lauds the black peasant roots of Richard Wright (in contrast to the petty bourgeois origins of Du Bois and James) and credits him with providing the most powerful existing black nationalist critique of Marxist theory in his fiction and essays. This account of Wright is nearly unintelligible to me. I find little sense of black collective insurgency in Wright's work; rather, it is an expression of individualistic revolt, taking the forms of violent assault or personal attack. This sense of revolt is based upon a self-contempt and even self-hatred, candidly acknowledged by one who has undergone intense de-humanization. Robinson's attempt to view Wright's Bigger Thomas in *Native Son* (1940) as anticipating Frantz Fanon's work in *The Wretched of the Earth* (1960) is also unconvincing—especially given the fact that Bigger murders not only the white woman Mary but also his black girlfriend Bessie. This is no move toward community but rather an atomistic assertion which negates any belief in affecting the powers that be through collective action with oppressed peoples. There are no such depictions of any such black collective agency in Wright's corpus—even in his powerful short stories, *Uncle Tom's Children*, written in the 1930s when he was a Communist Party member. Furthermore, Robinson's silence regarding Wright's later writings on African nationalism and black power—both devalued and demystified by Wright as props for the petty bourgeoisie—renders his argument even more vulnerable. In short, Robinson lauds a Richard Wright I simply don't recognize—a Wright who stands in sharp contrast to the basic drift of his corpus.

Despite my disagreements with Robinson's treatments of these three key figures of the black radical intellectual tradition and my skepticism about his search for *the* negation of capitalism (be it the proletariat or black radicalism), Robinson has written a major book that warrants serious scrutiny. His ultimate aim is to contribute to the freedom struggle of oppressed people by exploring the ways in which the Marxist tradition—indispensable for the struggle—may impede it through its Eurocentric focuses. The same holds true for patriarchal and homophobic people who, with dogmatism and false orthodoxy, refuse to deepen the Marxist tradition. Robinson's efforts make us recognize that this deepening in regard to race is the only avenue to follow if Marxism and black radicalism are to be vital in the years to come.

Notes

1. Leonard Harris, "Historical Subjects and Interests: Race, Class and Conflict," *The Year Left 2: An American Socialist Yearbook*, edited by Mike Davis, Manning Marable, et al. (London: Verso, 1987), pp. 90-105.

Rethinking Marxism

Harry Magdoff and Paul Sweezy are the most admired and beloved Marxists in the American Left community. As the co-editors of the major mainstay journal *Monthly Review*—as well as highly influential authors of pioneering books—they have played a fundamental role in shaping and molding radical thought and opinion among all generations of the left since the Second World War.

In *Rethinking Marxism: Struggles in Marxist Theory. Essays for Harry Magdoff and Paul Sweezy*, (New York: Autonomedia, 1985) editors Stephen Resnick and Richard Wolff have brought together an impressive array of Marxist intellectuals from around the world to pay tribute to Magdoff and Sweezy. The contributions include (among others) Samir Amin on the international capitalist crisis and the Third World; Rosalyn Baxandall and Elizabeth Ewen on contemporary feminism; Charles Bettelheim on class and class struggle in Marx; Samuel Bowles and Herbert Gintis on the labor theory of value; Andre Gunder Frank on Marx, Keynes, and *Monthly Review*; Elizabeth Fox-Genovese and Eugene Genovese on Frantz Fanon; Immanuel Wallerstein on Marx and underdevelopment; Ralph Miliband on capitalist democracy; David Levine's analysis of advanced capitalist economy; Donald Harris on value, exchange, and capital; and Ernest Mandel on commodity production and bureaucracy in Marx and Engels. In short, this book is an intellectual feast for any left reader.

Resnick and Wolff chose this occasion not only to honor Magdoff and Sweezy in the form of probing yet friendly essays by others, but also in the form of an introduction that provides a thorough epistemological critique of Marxist method and theory in the work of Sweezy and Magdoff. After a brief sketch of the pitfalls of rationalism and empiricism, they conclude:

Neither Sweezy nor Magdoff have chosen to address the matter of epistemological presumptions within Marxism and their consequences for the various formulations within the Marxist tradition. *Monthly Review* rarely if ever opened its pages to discussions or debates on these matters. Their proper and exemplary concern with empirical data was frequently extended unnecessarily into empiricist epistemological assertions. We find this regrettable.

What are Resnick and Wolff up to here? Why bring in such arcane considerations as epistemology? What is at stake in these matters? I suggest that their motivations can be understood in the following way. First, unlike Sweezy and Magdoff's task then and now (namely, to make Marxism and concrete Marxist analyses accessible to a *political* public), the aim of Resnick and Wolff is to intervene in an *academic* context wherein many emaciated and distorted Marxisms circulate for principally student/colleague consumption. Second, Resnick and Wolff rightly reject all forms of uncritical reductionist, crude determinist, and vulgar economistic versions of Marxism. This rejection leads them to reconstruct the most sophisticated formulation of Marxism in the academy in the past few years: Louis Althusser's complex and flexible view of Marxism which highlights the "overdetermined" character of social phenomena—that is, the fact that all aspects of society mutually and reciprocally affect one another.

For Resnick and Wolff, to be a sophisticated, i.e., epistemologically conscious, Marxist today is to be an overdeterminist who chooses class as a "theoretical entry point" for understanding social phenomena. This means that class is not to be viewed as an essential cause that accounts for all other aspects of society but rather as a methodological standpoint that accents both how class determines some aspects of society and how these aspects determine class.

On a deeper philosophic level, Resnick and Wolff hold that sophisticated Marxists must give up the notion that theory corresponds to or copies a "reality" or "set of facts" lying outside itself. Instead, Marxists should claim that theories constitute "reality" or predetermine what "set of facts" one will see. For Resnick and Wolff, to hold a correspondence theory of truth is to be a discredited epistemological realist and a naive essentialist. The badge of Marxist sophistication is that of anti-realism and anti-essentialism. So their major charge against Sweezy and Magdoff is that though they are superb Marxist social analysts, they remain tied to an outmoded epistemological stance.

To some, Resnick and Wolff's position seems to be that of an epistemological idealism; that is, they appear to hold that "reality" is a product of theory, that "facts" are effects of a particular method. Yet surely the realities of capital flight, the facts of the exploitation and devastation of workers under present-day multinational corporate capitalism are not mere products and effects of theories or methods. In reply, Resnick and Wolff would agree. For they argue that these realities and facts are *not created* by theories and methods, but rather are viewed, construed, and understood in light of our theories and methods. For example, bourgeois economists and social theorists would acknowledge capital flight and devastated lives of workers, but then seek to explain them as inevitable, given their allegiance to and defense of capitalist market forces. The crucial matter here is not idealism or realism in epistemology, but rather how we choose the theories and methods we use and how we justify such choices.

Sweezy and Magdoff could reply to Resnick and Wolff that the latters' sophisticated Marxism paves the way to an epistemological relativism—and possibly a familiar sociological pluralism of mutually interacting variables—that not only questions the scientific status of Marxism but also disarms its explanatory power. Resnick and Wolff would claim that epistemological relativism is inescapable, yet Marxism—with class as a "theoretical entry point" to understand and explain social phenomena—remains the best available theory we have.

This debate is noteworthy in that it makes Marxists more methodologically self-conscious. Yet it can become academic in the bad sense—self-absorptive and paralyzing—in that it may make little difference at the level of concrete social analysis. For instance, if one uses a flexible Marxist analysis that recognizes the impact of culture and the state on the economy yet still holds that the economy is more important in explaining culture and the state than vice versa, it matters little whether one needs the kind of avant-gardist epistemological academic credentials Resnick and Wolff celebrate. Such arcane epistemological matters become, to use Wittgenstein's apt phrase, "wheels that turn which do not affect the mechanism," i.e., are superfluous.

Ironically, this is seen most clearly in Resnick and Wolff's substantive essay in the volume on "A Marxian Reconceptualization of Income and Its Distribution," in which they put forward a subtle class analytical formulation that Sweezy and Magdoff could accept, independent of their different epistemological viewpoints. What then is it that makes a difference here—other than an academic soothing of the agonized epistemological consciences of anti-essentialist Marxists like Resnick and Wolff?

Unfortunately, the academy and its present epistemological obsessions have produced innocuous slogans like "essentialism" and "anti-essentialism" as though much were at stake. Yet, as Marx and Gramsci have taught us, the crucial levels of Marxism are those of concrete social and historical analysis and concrete political struggle. And if there is agreement on these levels—as there seems to be with Resnick and Wolff and Sweezy and Magdoff—the rest is academic. If there is disagreement, the crucial issue is not one's epistemology but rather the deployment of different concepts and their explanatory weight in accounting for concrete situations and projections for action. Resnick and Wolff rightly remind us not to succumb to anti-theoreticism or dogmatic methodologicism; but, I would add, we also must not bow to the empty epistemological obsessions rampant in avant-gardist circles in the bourgeois academy. Marxism is *acceptable* not because it is epistemologically sophisticated but because it provides the best explanations we have of the social misery we suffer or want to change. It will never become *respectable* in the academy as long as it holds to its goal of revolutionary transformation of capitalist societies. Like Resnick and Wolff, we must attack present-day emaciated and distorted Marxisms, but we must not divert and diffuse our precious energies in endless debates about who is more or less anti-essentialist.

As an African-American socialist Christian—whose "essentialism" is strategic and tactical rather than epistemic and foundational—I find this debate amusing in that I've always viewed Marxism first and foremost as neither a science—since that term has connotations of ideologies of expertise and managerial control that I abhor—nor as an arbitrary "theoretical point of entry." Rather I consider Marxism the best theoretical tradition initiated in Europe (given capitalism's Eurocentric origins) and now produced around the world that provides indispensable analytical weapons in my fight with and for the wretched of the earth.

In this regard, my motivations for adopting and deploying Marxist analyses are existential and moral. It is existential in that my existence as a black working class-bred human being *forced* me to come to terms with the ugly realities I could not possibly *not* know—cultural degradation, political oppression, and economic exploitation. It is moral in that I have a choice to side with cultural degraders, political rulers, and economic exploiters—as some black middle-class opportunists do. But I refuse to do so on moral and religious grounds. Marxism helps me keep track of and account for structural and institutional life-denying forces like degradation, oppression, and exploitation, and though I believe that the complexities of racism, sexism, and homophobia cannot be *fully* grasped in light of Marxism, they surely cannot be understood without it. In this way, the epistemology-centered debate of Resnick and Wolff obscures and obfuscates the role of one's own existential and moral orientations regarding why we take Marxism seriously in these postmodern times of skepticism, cynicism, and careerism. They come close to this when they state that "There is an irreducible autobiographical flavor to a Marxist's explanation of his/her choice of entry point or, for that matter, his/her commitment to overdetermination, the Marxist tradition, or anything else." But they never flesh this out, unpack it, or make it explicit.

In conclusion, *Rethinking Marxism* is a heartfelt gift to the two grand old men of Marxism in America and abroad. And, in all honesty, it is hard to think of the U.S. left scene without them. Yet we know that Sweezy and Magdoff cannot live forever. Resnick and Wolff have performed a great service in paying tribute to them by forcing us to re-examine Marxism and by reminding us that we must begin to prepare for how our left public sphere can preserve and build upon the rich fund of Marxist analyses, political struggle, and comradely love Sweezy and Magdoff have given us.

South Africa and Our Struggle

I would like to cast my presentation at three levels. The first has to do with the normative level—what kinds of values and norms emanate from the Christian tradition and what kind of resources can we cull from that tradition (as in South Africa and other places) that has been misused and distorted. In fact given this tradition, it takes tremendous audacity to be a Christian these days, especially in South Africa. What kind of demands, requirements, obligations, and duties flow therefrom?

The second level, the crucial level, deals with socio-economic analysis and with concrete institutional embodiments and the concrete social practices that flow from a particular socio-economic analysis. And the last level is that of action and praxis; that is to say, what kind of engagement can be enacted in light of the socio-economic analysis and based on the norms and values put forth from the Christian tradition?

The Normative Level

To be a progressive and prophetic Christian in the United States and South Africa, one has to speak to the personal level. Indeed, it has to do with issues of integrity, character and discipline. To be a Christian means to exemplify what one espouses. It is precisely a personal issue of integrity because it is quite easy to talk and engage in rhetoric without seriously coming to terms with what one espouses. This is especially true in the United States where commitment becomes a kind of commodity. Thus commitment-talk becomes fashionable. In contrast, this is not the case in South Africa where commitment means ultimately contemplating the loss of one's life.

Moreover, we have to talk seriously about what kind

of very profound levels of risk and sacrifice are necessary. Specifically, we speak of courage, the basic act of placing the needs of others over and beyond that of oneself. Oftentimes, especially in prophetic discourse, we tend to skip over this moment. Rather, we need to particularly highlight it given the situation of our brothers and sisters in South Africa. Because they have to deal with it every day. We in the United States tend to hold personal sacrifice at arms' length because we do not have the repressive state apparatus staring us in the face as directly and immediately as do the brothers and sisters in apartheid South Africa.

Thus the issue of courage and sacrifice challenges our Christian faith. What does it mean to be a Christian in a context in which class, racial and gender contradictions (e.g., social institutional sins) are so intense, overwhelming and pervasive that it might require giving up one's life? To attempt an answer to such a profound personal and existential dilemma, we turn to the normative level. Out of the Christian tradition, I would like to emphasize three notions, norms or values.

The first is the notion of the *imago dei,* a very traditional notion: to be made in the image of God; to spotlight the sanctity and the dignity of individuals. All individuals are unique and made in God's image and thereby warrant a certain kind of treatment. This is very important because it relates to the universalism and the egalitarianism of the Christian gospel. I would suggest that *imago dei,* in the present situation, has subversive implications. It has revolutionary implications. Though it sounds like a simple theological point, it, in fact, diametrically opposes the hierarchical structures that we see shot through societies such as the United States and South Africa.

The second notion is "fallenness." Fallenness does not have a popular status because it deals with the whole classical formulations of sin. As Christians, however, we should take very seriously sin on the personal and institutional levels. In fact, a serious grappling with sin allows me to arrive at very radical democratic values. For example, the abuse of power is inherent in excessive power; absolute power corrupts absolutely. Therefore, we need accountability mechanisms to thwart such a sin. We need radical democratic institutions to account for all forms of power and to maintain checks and balances, not simply in the political sphere, but in the economic and the cultural also.

"Kingdom-talk" or the coming of the Kingdom, the last notion, responds to what I consider to be the most fundamental issue in talking about South Africa and the United States. For Christians, that is the problem of evil; how does one respond to and resist the forms of evil, institutional evil especially. Thus Kingdom-talk provides a means of, on the one hand, sustaining some sense of meaning in a meaningless situation. And most important, on the other hand, it allows one to undergo empowerment in a situation in which one feels relatively powerless.

Kingdom-talk offers, then, a way by which the in-breaking of the Kingdom into the present sustains hope for those undergoing a struggle against overwhelming odds, and offers a source of empowerment in a situation in which the power seems to reside on the surface among those elites, among the ruling classes who deploy the most repressive terroristic means of regulating the population.

In summary, three notions occupy the normative level—the *imago dei*, fallenness, and the Kingdom's coming.

The Level of Social Analysis

I would like to spend much more time on the second level, the level of social analysis. I cannot stress enough how important social analysis is in understanding the operations of the multi-level, multi-dimensional operations of power; that is, how one understands wealth, prestige, status, influence and how these circulate in a particular society. Indeed, I would go so far as to argue that most of the battles within the Christian tradition these days have to do with battles over social analysis. For instance, all Christians today seem to be for freedom, equality, and democracy. Yes, but the question is how do you interpret these claims; what is the analytical content and substance of these assertions? The analytical content and substance are supplied by one's social analysis. As Christians, we wish to employ social analysis from the vantage point of society's victims, from the vantagepoint of those who suffer, from the vantagepoint of the Cross, the Christocentric perspective. Therefore the types of social analyses we would deploy not only attempt to interpret the world but also attempt to isolate potentialities for ultimate realization in struggle.

Accordingly, we must note that our overall discursive context is a battle. Here is one of the few places I agree with John Calvin: human history is in fact a battleground for struggle, contestation, conflict, and resistance. The question is not only on what side are you but also how you understand the side that you are on such that you can ultimately triumph. The aim is to win, to expand the scope of democracy, to expand the scope of individuals who have a status of sanctity and dignity. In this sense, social analysis is a weapon, a tool, an instrument for struggle. This is very important because a lot of our secular comrades, especially on the left, tend to make social analysis and tools of social analysis themselves fetishes and idols. Whereas, for Christians, social analyses serve simply as tools and instruments.

Social and historical analyses aid us in historically situating and locating a people at a particular moment. Where is the struggle in South Africa at this particular moment? Where is the struggle in the United States at this particular moment? In response, I would like to begin with the "Europeanization of the world." In particular, we live at the end of the age of Europe which began roughly in 1492 and ended in 1945. And, of course, post-1945 World War II is the start of the American century. The century only lasted for 28 years, from 1945 to 1973, but, nonetheless, post-World War II US ascendancy marked the beginning of an American century. The "Europeanization of the world" and the American century serve as historical backdrops in our comprehending the tremendous resurgence of insurgency and resistance in the United States (principally black-led in the 1950s with Martin Luther King, Jr.) and, of course, the tremendous insurgency in South Africa post-World War II (symbolically best represented by the June 16th Soweto Student Rebellion).

What exactly do I mean by the "Europeanization of the world"? I designate particular institutional life-denying forces with a global and international scope. More specifically, I would characterize them as exploitation, domination, repression, and subjugation. Oftentimes, we utilize these terms in an interchangeable manner. But I suggest that they are not identical and synonymous at all. True, they inseparably connect in the concrete world in which we live. Yet for analytical purposes, we can distinguish them. Here our social and historical analyses provide a means to engage these four institutional forms of evil which confront Americans and South Africans as children of God struggling for freedom and liberation.

Economic Exploitation

The first, economic exploitation, deals with the emergence of the capitalist mode of production. Here Marxist analysis becomes indispensable (as we shall see, I think, it is ultimately inadequate; but it is indispensable). Marxist analysis acts as one of the essential components in a Christian understanding of institutional forms of evil. In other words, we cannot understand the Europeanization of the world without understanding the emergence of the capitalist mode of production and the impact that it has had on victims in the world, specifically for our purposes, on people of African descent. The capitalist mode of production attempts to extend its scope around the globe. A graphic example: in 1834, European powers owned 35 percent of the land on the globe. By 1918, they controlled 87 percent of the land on the globe.

But what do we mean by the capitalist mode of production? This historically-constituted mode of production signifies classes being formed in social relations of production. It signifies a minority owning the land and the instruments of production and forcing the majority to work, to sell its labor power, and to sell its time and energy and skills to those who own that land and instruments of production. Thus capital, in this sense, is not mere money or revenue. It is a *social* relation shot through with relative powerlessness of workers. At this juncture, we discover a major misunderstanding by the majority of Americans. Even as they live lives of prosperity, most Americans live lives of relative powerlessness.

Consequently, living in a capitalist society by definition suggests a life of material insecurity, precisely because you have no control over the conditions of your work place. For example, small farmers in rural Oklahoma believed they lived lives of prosperity until the structural shift in capitalism threw them onto the anarchic market. We could say the same thing about workers in Norwood, Ohio, who were informed that General Motors planned to close. Of course we could say the same thing about the large numbers of unemployed persons in South Africa whom the ruling class utilizes as a reserve labor army to ensure low wages and also to militaristically control the South African labor force.

Hence a Marxist analysis of the capitalist mode of production proves indispensable in determining which movements we will join and in comprehending the maldistribution of wealth in South Africa and the United States. The maldistribution of wealth supersedes the common sense notion of how many swimming pools and big houses one owns (i.e., in white Johannesburg). Yes, that is one manifestation. But my analysis of wealth speaks to the fundamental structural impediments and constraints for property and holdings. Part of the problem, especially in the United States, lies with our definition of wealth. We tend to think of income rather than holdings, earnings rather than property holdings. In fact most of the economic data one finds pinpoint how much money people make. But that is not wealth. Wealth involves ownership. Even the American middle class does not own much. They might have credit cards that allow a certain lifestyle, but they do not own much. The picture focuses more clearly when we turn to South Africa. But we should not think that the U.S. has a more equitable or egalitarian distribution of wealth. On the contrary, the U.S. capitalist pie is so large that a number of persons are able to share it and call themselves middle-class when they are actually workers, exploited by the capitalist system.

Again, a social analysis of capitalist economic exploitation is crucial. Here we must guard against classifying exploitation as simply a moral term. Marx's *Kapital* makes a great contribution in clarifying this when his work defines exploitation as a relation that results in relative powerlessness. Far from a mere finger-pointing moral critique, exploitation involves an analytic interpretation of the structural constraints of distributing wealth that results in a small number of people monopolizing tremendous wealth and the majority of persons having little wealth at all.

State Repression

The second level of the Europeanization of the world deals with state repression. The people of African descent know state repression quite well. For instance, black people in the southern USA had to undergo crypto-fascist institutionalized terrorism for over 250 years; lynching being one of the most salient examples of institutionalized terrorism. Thus state repression represents the deployment of the repressive state apparatus in order to control persons. It links principally to the military, to the army, to the prisons, to the police, etc. Though state repression is inseparable from economic exploitation, it is not the same thing. It maintains its own relative autonomy. However, ultimately the ruling elites in the economic sphere of society influence the state. In this instance, Michael Foucault's works help us to come to terms with forms of state repression: surveillance, torture, and disciplinary control.

Bureaucratic Domination

"Bureaucratic domination," the third level of the Europeanization of the world, is very important because it permeates both capitalist modes of production as well as state repressive apparatuses.

Furthermore, because they are hierarchical, bureaucracies entail rhetorics of submission and subordination. (At the same time, we should always note the historically determined nature of all bureaucracies. In other words, they do not have to contain their present hierarchical state.) Thus today's bureaucracies construct various ways to check people's power. Not only do political movements become bureaucratized themselves, but they also suffer from bourgeois bureaucracies that diffuse and dilute their energies in an attempt to suck off the people's leadership and incorporate that leadership into these intentionally lethargic bourgeois institutions. These bureaucracies claim efficiency; that was the ideological justification for modern forms of bureaucracy that Max Weber analyzed. But in reality, we know that the basic aim of bureaucracy is self-perpetuation. Again, they have their own relative autonomy.

So far we have touched upon economic exploitation and its relation to profit maximization, the political sphere (on the state) and its relation to controlling the instrumentalities of violence (as well as the institutions of public administration), and bureaucratic domination and its relation to self-perpetuity.

Subjugation

We now come to "subjugation," the final manifestation of the Europeanization of the world. Subjugation concerns racism (so fundamental in both histories of the USA and South Africa), sexism, homophobia, etc. Subjugation concerns the social and historical construction of particular identities and subjectivities; which is to say issues of self-perception or self-image or, what Marcus Garvey called, "identity." This plays a crucial role in grasping various socio-political movements because the way in which you view yourself is one of the means by which you acquire empowerment.

For instance in American history, the identity issue pervades in the construction of the Negro subject as opposed to black subjects, African subjects as opposed to Afro-American subjects. Garvey understood the significance of identity. It is no accident that he led the largest mass movement in the United States. Indeed, the cultural resources and the sense of cultural agency (e.g., identity) are inseparable from the political agency. How you conceive yourself is inseparable from what you perceive yourself doing politically. Therefore, the degree to which you understand yourself as degraded, inferior, and subordinate precludes and forecloses political possibilities for how you will act. Similarly, how you view yourself as not only a child of God but also as an African with a proud heritage, past, and history, affects how you think about the future and how you act in the present.

In summary, all four examples of institutional evil are part and parcel of the appropriate social analysis needed by Christians. The first level of evil principally relates to Marx (e.g., economic exploitation). The second level principally relates to Foucault (e.g., state repression). The third principally relates to Weber (e.g., bureaucratism). And the fourth relates to Garvey, Angela Davis and Malcolm X (e.g., anti-racist and anti-sexist subjugation). All four go hand-in-hand.

The Praxis Level

In dealing with the "present socio-political-economic movements for change," so far we have explored the normative and social analysis levels. We now reach the final section, the level of praxis.

Aristotle argued that the conclusion of a practical syllogism was not a resolution but an action. I would want to argue that it is the same in any analysis for Christians. More specifically, if one does not ultimately talk about engaging in action and praxis, then one's talk is academic; it is simply discursive as opposed to political action. Thus the question becomes: in what possible actions and potential practices can one engage? Of course the contexts of the United States and South Africa are, on the one hand, inseparable, and, on the other, different.

First a look at South Africa. In that country, we see those movements that are against economic exploitation and therefore are radically anti-capitalist. We see those movements that are against state repression and thereby are anti-repressive state apparatus, that are in fact anti-hierarchical. And therefore, they are concerned about democratizing the bureaucratic institutions. Lastly, we see those movements that are fundamentally anti-subjugation which means that they are anti-racist and anti-sexist.

What kinds of movements does one then attempt to put forward? A lot depends on the weight placed on each of the four institutional evils elaborated above. In other words, if one views capitalist economic exploitation at the center of evil, then one's political movement will primarily focus on economic exploitation. However, if one surmises identity as the principal evil, then one's energies will stress the importance of the Africa identity in a white dominated world. Here issues of black consciousness and black positive identity will come to the center.

In my judgment, one encounters one of the most salutary developments in South Africa when one observes most resistance movements interweaving all four kinds of institutional evils in their analysis. Whether one speaks of the Azanian Peoples' Organization (AZAPO) or the United Democratic Front (UDF), all posit a holistic analysis against evil.

Given the necessity for an integrated approach to institutional evils, what should be the proper Christian response to economic exploitation, state repression, bureaucratic domination, and racist (and sexist) subjugation? I would want to argue for two basic options for South Africa. First, one could undertake various kinds of community actions characterized by mobilizing and organizing blacks and progressive whites. Finally, there exists the church's attempt to not play a "third role." I like the *Kairos Document's* critique of the church's false belief in its ability to stand above the fray and mediate as if the very conflict itself has not already penetrated and divided the church. No, the church has to take a stand. It has to choose in such a way that it preserves its Christian identity; yet that Christian identity itself does not become a fetish. On the one hand, Christians must uphold their Christian identity while entering social movements and political organizations. On the other hand, a Christian should not become so preoccupied with one's Christian self that it separates him/her from the social struggle.

Armed Struggle

What potentialities exist for the first option of armed struggle and guerrilla warfare? First, we should acknowledge the current existence of armed struggle. But it is weak and feeble given the situation of the strength of the South African state. Nevertheless, guerrilla warfare tragically exemplifies a symptom of just how deep the evil is. Indeed, Christians who wish to speak of a just war or just rebellion or just revolution would have to have a very deep doctrine of evil and sin and how to combat such sin.

Second, I think highly of the pacifist tradition in Christendom. I do not agree with it; I am not persuaded by it. But I think it is respectful. I do not think Christian pacifists will ever have the kind of impact on history that many of them would purport to have. Yet I respect their views. So when I hear Archbishop Tutu or Allan Boesak and many others argue for non-violence, I respect them. Furthermore, without doubt, one should, on principled ground, attempt to exercise and realize all forms of non-violent resistance before one even entertains the discussion of violent resistance and armed struggle. Then we have to look at the history of a country and see what possibilities have there been for non-violent resistance and what impact non-violent resistance has had. If we, in fact, discover that non-violent resistance in its most noble form has been crushed mercilessly by the rulers, then it raises the possibility of forced engagement in armed struggle. Indeed, this is no way alien to the Christian tradition. For instance, the Christian elemetns of the ruling class of the United States claims that the American Revolutionary War, the Civil War, World War I, World War II, the Korean War, and the Vietnam War were all necessary and Christian. Yet, when black folk begin to think of armed struggle, the white ruling elite responds: "well, we've got some complex problems we've got to come to terms with before we even entertain the possibility of armed self-defense." It is this type of intellectual arrogance (and racism) that one has to resist.

But, on the other hand, one should never view armed struggle as a plaything. One should not romanticize or idealize it at all. On the contrary, one should carefully and thoroughly think through whether it can have the impact and effectiveness that one desires. Specifically for South Africa, that means weighing relations with neighboring countries; whether there will be space and support from them.

In my estimation, if the majority of South Africans reach the conclusion that all forms of non-violent resistance have been called into question (that, in fact, the current civil war requires self-defensive violent resistance as well as ultimate transformative violent resistance), then it is incumbent upon Christians in the First World not only to support that kind of activity but also to provide understanding of it to other people in the First World. We witnessed this process in the 1960s as Africa underwent decolonization. Likewise this last bastion of Afrikaner colonization will require the same kind of solidarity and support from Christians and people of goodwill as those in the 1960s did for Ghana, Kenya, and other African nations.

However, South Africa, it seems to me, is in many ways still far removed from a situation in which effective armed struggle and guerrilla warfare can be waged. It might, indeed, be on the agenda in the next fifteen or twenty years. But today, a variety of different obstacles impede violent resistance, such as: the destabilization of neighboring African countries by the South African government; and the role the United States could play both covertly and explicitly in its support for the apartheid state against such resistance.

Mobilization and Organization

Because armed struggle ultimately depends upon how well one relates to the masses of people, we next move to mobilization and organization. One cannot simply emerge and commence fighting. For instance, I think the tremendous courage and heroism that we see in South Africa among the young folk (particularly since their 1984 student revolt) has to do with a political impatience. But political impatience differs from thoroughly thought-out strategy and tactics, thoroughly thought-out mobilization and organization. You need that subversive energy of the youth and students if you are going to have strategy and tactics. But sheer political impatience, in and of itself, can result in becoming mere cannon fodder for the repressive state apparatus in South Africa.

Therefore the question becomes organizing and mobilization which relates to consciousness. By consciousness, I am suggesting orientation and direction and convincing persons regarding credible alternatives. People will not engage in a revolutionary leap of faith until they, on the one hand, see such acts of valor and courage manifest (which has been the case in South Africa) and, on the other hand, are convinced of the lack of other credible alternatives. There is still a deep problem of conscientizing the masses in South Africa, it seems to me. Black South Africans do not comprise a monolithic or homogeneous bloc.

Consequently, in that context one has to develop religious and ideological contestation. And the organizing and mobilizing would target this ongoing conscientization process: at the cultural level of identity, African heritage, overcoming the racist self-perception; at the level of the economic sphere in terms of what particular form capitalism takes in South Africa in exploiting the majority of the population; and in the political sphere in terms of the rule of law. "Rule of law" sounds like liberalism, but liberalism at its best is an indispensable element in any socialist vision or any egalitarian vision. Why? Because liberalism connotes equal status before the law, one-person-one-vote, which in South Africa today is subversive. The protection of rights and liberties (e.g., liberalism) remains basic.

In summary, conscientization must proceed in the political, economic and cultural spheres. And Christian churches have the obligation to participate in that kind of conscientization, given the previously mentioned resources of *imago dei*, made equal in the image of God; of fallenness and therefore the need for accountability structures and radical democratic mechanisms; and of this coming Kingdom or Kingdom-talk, this unquenchable quest for freedom.

The Christian Church

I would like to end by noting the role of Christian churches. In a sense, we in the United States need the energies of the masses of South Africa. We in the United States currently suffer a profound demoralization. The pacification of our communities by drugs and alcohol, by the cultural industry of television and radio, and by music saps our energies that could be used for change.

However, all of us are caught in addiction and stimulation of some sort. But the black and brown communities receive concentrations of the more deadly, demonic forms. Therefore demoralization and pacification set in. As a result, it makes it very difficult for leaders to emerge, to be courageous. To be courageous, one has to step out by oneself. Today that is much more difficult than it was in the 1960s when more people were stepping out alongside you. Again, in that sense, this leadership vacuum is something that we black folk in the United States, we Africans in the United States have to take very seriously and to learn from the progressive stand taken by Christians who support the *Kairos Document*. Clearly, now is the time for the church's role to be prophetic, persuasive and pacesetting; that is, in the interests of the poor against perpetrators of exploitation, domination, repression, and subjugation.

The Struggle for America's Soul

The decline and decay of the nation's institutions has shaken the confidence of many Americans, who now fear they have little capacity to solve social problems. The shattering of families, neighborhoods and schools has extinguished hope. The avalanche of everyday violence, escalating economic inequality and ecological devastation—along with crumbling highways, subways, bridges and buildings—has led to despair, cynicism and apathy.

Robert N. Bellah, a sociologist at the University of California, and his four collaborators—Ann Swidler, Richard Madsen, William M. Sullivan and Steven M. Tipton—attempt to address the crisis in American institutions in their new work, *The Good Society*. This sequel to their influential 1985 book, *Habits of the Heart: Individualism and Commitment in American Life,* comes at a crucial moment. In common with the movement toward democracy in countries throughout the world, the authors believe, Americans can find new purpose and identity in revitalizing and transforming their own institutions.

Habits of the Heart was largely a critique of American individualism as expressed in the lives of the white middle class. The book analyzed the impoverished ways in which most Americans pursue the good life, and attempted, in the authors' words, "to find a moral language that will transcend...radical individualism." Those readers who were dismayed by the often superficial analysis in that book should give the sequel a chance. Instead of refueling the old, tired academic debate between orthodox liberals who champion individual rights and romantic communitarians who promote civic responsibility, Mr. Bellah and his colleagues highlight the complex relationship of individuals and institutions in a democratic society. *The Good Society* is, in fact, a passionate inquiry about the struggle for

America's soul, a struggle that points toward a renewed democratic identity and egalitarian mission, rooted in an understanding of the true nature of institutions and the relationship of citizens to them.

The authors' focus on individual fulfillment and citizen participation echoes John Dewey's response to Walter Lippmann's indictment of democracy in *Public Opinion* (1922) and *The Phantom Public* (1925). In these two significant books, Lippmann argued that popular participation in public affairs should be circumscribed because of citizens' limited knowledge and their tendency toward hedonistic distraction. In *The Public and Its Problems* (1927), Dewey gave new life to the old saying that the cure for the ills of democracy is more democracy. Although *The Good Society* takes its title from a Lippmann book published in 1937, Mr. Bellah and his colleagues side with Dewey, even as they lament the paucity of such debates between public philosophers in our day.

The writers' goal is to enrich the quality of American life by invigorating the American people. Their book links democratic reform to personal transformation; it connects the ways in which we govern ourselves to the ways we live our lives. Indeed, the central value of democracy is understood by the authors not only as a form of self-government, but also as a way of life.

The authors state bluntly that "a good society is one in which attention takes precedence over distraction"; that means, for example, choosing family and children over personal indulgence, or choosing environmental and civic concern over private opulence. Yet such attention depends on what Mr. Bellah and his colleagues call a new "pattern of cultivation"—a deep sense of history combined with a subtle moral sensibility—in order to give purpose and meaning to both individual and social life.

In a powerful concluding chapter, "Democracy Means Paying Attention," Mr. Bellah and his colleagues hope to persuade us to pay attention to the institutions that support us. The authors write that "paying attention is how we use our psychic energy, and how we use our psychic energy determines the kind of self we are cultivating, the kind of person we are learning to be... The nature of the institutions we both inhabit and transform has much to do with our capacity to sustain attention... Institutions are socially organized forms of paying attention or attending, although they can also, unfortunately, be socially organized forms of distraction."

The book advances a series of powerful critiques of the kind of corporate, political, educational and religious leadership that stifles innovation and penalizes boldness. And it provides an insightful overview of the ways in which American institutions of all kinds—from the church to the corporation—promote citizens' passivity and reinforce their personal distractions.

"At least some of our citizens have come to see that the present organization of our economic life, including the corporation, threatens not only our democratic government, because of its inordinate political influence, but also our national character and form of life, because of its propagation of the idea of wealth as merely the accumulation of consumer goods," they write. Since "market forces are rapidly invading every sphere of society," the authors say, an institutional response—not simply an individualistic one—is necessary. Despite their description of an erosion of trust in American institutions that has left citizens apathetic and cynical, Mr. Bellah and his collaborators reject the notion that the best American democracy has to offer is a coterie of experts beholden to politicians who are, in turn, influenced by corporate and financial elites.

But like most prophets of participatory democracy, including Dewey, Mr. Bellah and his colleagues are short on strategy. Echoing Vaclav Havel, they call for a politics of trust to replace a politics of fear. Yet the authors are reluctant to speak directly of Americans' diverse fears: of women, homosexuals, labor, Latinos, Native Americans,

Jews and, especially, black people. Are these fears not tearing us apart—over women's rights in Wichita, sexual orientation in Greenwich Village, race in Los Angeles and Milwaukee, race and religion in Crown Heights? The book suggests that perhaps "a new social movement is called for," yet the authors do not tell us who will constitute this movement. They know that it must be a multiracial affair, but they give us no clue as to how this coming together can take place, or what will hold such a movement together.

The moral vision of the authors is commendable, their motives noble, their analysis subtle. Yet their prophetic jeremiad is slightly out of touch with the inchoate, scattered yet gathering progressive movement that is emerging across the American landscape. This gathering now lacks both the vital moral vocabulary and the focused leadership that can constitute and sustain it. Yet it will be rooted ultimately in current activities by people of color, by labor and ecological groups, by women, by gays and lesbians. These activities do not receive serious examination in this book.

Mr. Bellah and his collaborators rightly recognize that there can be no such progressive project in American society without arriving at a higher moral ground. Yet for such a project to take hold in the messy world of politics, people and power, our feet must also be firmly on the ground—especially when conservatives have claimed so much of it for so long. This book's vigorous defense of participatory democracy, much like Dewey's in the 1920s, may appear to be a voice crying in the wilderness; *The Good Society* reminds us that the wilderness, however seductive, should not be mistaken for the promised land.

The Crisis in Black America

I think this gathering is very important, because we are at a period now with the black situation where if we don't come together at least to reflect, the state of siege raging in black America will continue to swallow up our children, will continue to debilitate our sense of possibility and will continue to push us up against the wall in such a way that there may not even be a black America in 50 years...because we will be so scattered and disbursed, in prisons and coffins.

Now I was told by my close friend from Ward that at eleven o'clock tomorrow morning...Sunday at eleven o'clock in the morning, the great Nelson Mandela will be released unconditionally. They are already dancing in the streets in South Africa. Those of us rooted in the Christian tradition would say, God is still at work. God's people are still on the move. This ought to be a source of inspiration for those of us who are freedom fighters here in the United States and that the South African movement that has served in so many ways in sustaining us will continue to do so even more so given the kind of vision that Nelson Mandela will now be able to articulate outside of those prisons that have held him captive for over 27 years.

Let me turn then to the subject, "The Crisis in Black America." I want to begin first by saying something about Black History Month. I was talking to Rev. Epps this morning and it was music to my ears to hear him say that here's an institution that wants to go far beyond the recounting of black achievements and accomplishments. It wants to go beyond nostalgic celebration. It wants to go beyond cathartic expression about the great things and deeds and undergoings that black people have been able to put forth over the last 300 years or so. And I think this is so very important that we have to be able to move into a mode of critical history—not monumental or antiquarian history.

By critical history, what I mean is looking at the present as history and looking at the way in which the past has fundamentally shaped and molded that present—the pastness of the present and the pastness in the present...why?...because this is the only way that we can think seriously about projecting imaginatively a future. Antiquarian history relics in a museum is a dead tradition, stagnant, stationary.

Monumental history romanticizes and idealizes as if every black person was a Frederick Douglass and every leader was a Martin Luther King, Jr. and every freedom fighter was an Ella Baker. No, there have been defeats. There has been ignorance. There has been silliness and pettiness in our history. There have been profound lack of insight and weaknesses in our history just as there have been visionaries and ordinary black folk working every day, holding up a blood-stained banner in such a way that the next generation would be able to forge more space. So when we look at our past, we don't fantasize, we don't idealize, but we also don't succumb to the narrow views that we have done nothing. Somewhere in between we struggled, we've won, we've lost, we've cried, we've laughed, we've had joy, we've had peace and sorrow. It is not a history solely of oppression, but great damage has been done. It is not a history solely of resistance, but some victories have been won.

What I want to do this morning is to look at the present as history to give us some sense of where we are and then to end with some strategies and tactics of where we are to go. As I said when I first stepped up to this podium...it seems to me that black America is now in the most critical moment that it has ever been since we arrived on these shores. I want to tell you why. The reason is that because this country is in one of its most critical moments since it conceived of itself as a nation in 1776.

We can't talk about Black History unless you talk

about American History, unless you talk about Modern History—because it's not just human beings of a darker hue who are struggling, but we're struggling against something. And we are struggling for what we need, which is more resources in order to live decent lives. If there is a common denominator of Black History, it is that black people have had relative difficulty in gaining access to resources—not enough housing, not enough health-care, not enough education. But also cultural resources in terms of how we conceive of ourselves—not enough positive self-images, not enough self-esteem, not enough self-respect, not enough self-affirmation of our capacity and potentiality...that's a resource too. And the problem is, how do we gain access to these resources. Two hundred and forty-four years of slavery did not allow us to gain too much, but we did have enough to keep going. That's a part of the strength that we ought to gain when we look at the struggle of our foremothers and forefathers under those conditions of perpetual and inheritable domination of slavery.

But this quest for resources in a nation that presently is in deep crisis...what do I mean by a nation in deep crisis? What I mean by it is...first, America is a first-class military power becoming a second-class economic power and in a stage of cultural decay and decline. Think about that—tremendous military power, but losing more and more economically to the Japanese and West Germans and others, and culturally you can't walk the streets at night. That's decay. It's decline. It's deterioration. It's a high level of criminality and so forth and so on. And America finds itself caught within these worlds. Black Americans find themselves caught within these whirlwinds, because we are a part of it. The worst of the situation is in terms of the difficulty of access to resources. Indigenous people are also on the bottom...they have less resources than we do. Black America has a middle class that can fill a whole host of churches, and indigenous people don't. Twenty-eight percent of black Americans are in the middle class. But we are the symbol of being on the bottom, because we are an integral part of this society in a way in which indigenous brothers and sisters are not. Tragically, indigenous peoples' reservations are marginalized, invisible. We are the symbol of being on the bottom. And so when you think about our crisis, we have to acknowledge the fact that this country at this particular moment still is struggling with two brutal and undeniable facts of its history in relation to us. One is that this is a profoundly conservative society. What I mean by that is it is a chronically racist society. It is chronically sexist. It is chronically homophobic, and it is chronically chauvinistic in its views of how it understands its patriotism and nationalism. Now what do I mean by that? What I mean by that is that in America human beings define themselves physically, socially, politically and sexually in terms of whiteness and blackness, in terms of maleness and femaleness, in terms of heterosexuality and homosexuality, and in terms of American and un-American. This is how we perceive of ourselves, and it reinforces constraints on the human capacities of those who are victimized by the racism, the sexism, the homophobia and the chauvinism.

To be defined as un-American in America usually, up until the present, meant Communist or socialist. Most freedom fighters are called Communist or socialist. They even called Martin Luther King a Communist or socialist. Why?...because he was a freedom fighter in the best way he knew how. But this is one example. We won't even talk about the discourse of whiteness and blackness in America. And never forget that when Italians and Irish and Lithuanians arrived in America, they didn't know they were white. The Italians thought they were Italians. They learned they were white by looking at us which meant that's, in part, how they became Americans, because there is no discourse of whiteness and blackness in the southern part of Italy. They were on the way to becoming Americans. This is how we have shaped the national identity of the country and usually articulated in a *conservative* way. But the first brutal fact.

The second brutal fact is that this is a country whose outlook, whose interest, is fundamentally shaped by big business. When Calvin Coolidge said that the business of America is business, he meant the business of America is big business. And think of the relation of corporations and their rights to the struggle of black people. The Fourteenth Amendment was designed to protect the rights of black people, to protect the rights of ex-slaves. But in 1886 one of the most crucial decisions which occurred in the history of this country is called *Santa Clara County vs. The Pacific Railroad*. What it decided was that a corporation is a person, and what it claimed then was that the corporation's rights could be protected under the Fourteenth Amendment that was intended for us. And between 1890 and 1910 there were nineteen cases presented before the Supreme Court that related to us, and there were 288 cases before the Supreme Court that related to the corporations-as-person, to protect their property, their treatment of workers, their control of the labor process—the period of the robber barons...unregulated economic accumulation at the expense of working people. And what we are talking about, then, is a vast maldistribution of resources of the wealth in the nation.

At this very moment one percent of Americans own 32 percent of the wealth. Think about that. I'm not talking about income, because if you're talking about income, your describing what people have to work for week in and week out. I'm talking about wealth. I'm talking about holdings—not earnings. It comes through stock dividends. But most of us do worry about earnings. Even if you think you are doing alright as a middle class person, let that check miss you a couple of months, and you will see how much holdings you have.

You understand what I'm talking about? I'm concerned about students as well here. I'm so glad to see them here. So unjust maldistribution of wealth makes it difficult for those on the bottom, as it were, to have assets. Think about it. Forty-five percent of Americans own two percent of the wealth. Now see, most of us are part of that. Owing to what?...the tremendous influence of big business—that the fundamental linchpin of this nation has been economic growth by means of corporate priorities. I'm gonna say that again—economic growth by means of corporate priorities.

So when we look at the economy presently in light of the black plight and predicament, what do we see? 1945 was the end of the age of Europe, right? It was the end of the Second World War...those ugly concentration camps in Europe, those mushroom clouds over Nagasaki and Hiroshima. The United States for the first time moved to the center of the historical stage. For the first time it is an uncontested and unchallenged world power. Europe is in devastation, a divided continent, needing a Marshall Plan in order to sustain it, and USSR controlling its eastern side after Yalta '45. 1945 was a period in which the United States begins its unprecedented economic boom, creating for the first time in human history a mass middle class, which is to say a society whose social structure looks like a diamond rather than a pyramid. Most social structures look like a pyramid—the majority on the bottom and a very few at the top.

What we see in America between 1945 and 1973 is the diamond, with a majority in the middle, minority on the bottom and minority at the top. It is during this period for the first time that black people are able, owing to blood, sweat and tears of activists, visionaries, leaders and followers to begin to make some entrée into that middle class. The Civil Rights Movement was in part a movement of black folk including themselves within that middle class as the economy was expanding at the expense of U.S. domination in Latin America, at the expense of a Marshall Plan which was U.S. domination of Europe. The pie was getting bigger, but it was not being redistributed. It was getting bigger, and after tremendous blood, sweat and tears, we get a foothold in the middle class. We get a foothold in the working class, especially the industrial class of those working in automobile factories in Detroit. The Barry Gordies and the Smokey Robinsons began as workers in Detroit and then broke and became entrepreneurs and created one of the grand cultural productions in this country. We will talk about culture a little bit later. The rubber workers in Akron, the steel workers in Pittsburgh, some black entrée into what?...access to resources, wages. Why?...because we had been working in the south in the fields, and as their business began mechanize agricultural labor, they didn't need us any longer, we moved to the cities looking for jobs. Some came to California from Alabama, Oklahoma, Louisiana—looking for jobs usually tied to the public sphere, usually tied to the armed forces and the post offices because the private sphere, for the most part, wouldn't hire us in the 30s and 40s. But the point here is that the economic boom stopped in 1973, you see. There was a contraction in the economy. Why was it?...because there was fierce competition from the West Germans and the Japanese, because there was a takeover of monopoly of oil production of OPEC.

Remember the lines in the 70s? Texas and Oklahoma used to dominate the oil industry, but OPEC organized and took over. It's also because the internal, international debt structure became so fragile because the banks were making tremendous loans to third world countries and felt more and more dependent on these loans, given the fact that the third world countries began to think maybe they won't pay them back. But contraction occurred, and it is here where conservatism set in—an onslaught and assault on black working people began. It was an onslaught that had tremendous implications. It took the form of de-industrialization of industrial plants moving to the Third World. It took the form of a consolidation of a business class so that it was able to support politicians that could enact policies of vast cutback in social programs, of vast take-backs at the negotiation table between employers and employees, which means cutbacks in benefits. It took the form of vast layoffs of persons so that the unemployment rates became incredible—not just in black America, but especially in black America.

Now, the implication of this in terms of our politics is very important. It is very important indeed, because it meant then that this occurred right at the time when we are making entrée—not just into the middle class, but into politics as elected officials, as mayors, in the state legislatures and so forth. During this period we find our elected black officials, many of them eloquent and courageous, under tremendous constraints. They come to office and their tax bases are eroding. They come to office and they have very little assets to revenue, because the middle classes with money have moved out and the corporations are threatening to leave if they are not given privileged status. That's why Detroit looks like it does under the leadership of Coleman Young. Coleman Young can talk as much as he wants, but Mr. Ford's Ford Company still holds much of the destiny of Detroit in his hands, which means Coleman is to some extent still in Mr. Ford's hands. The same is true with Mr. Bradley here in Los Angeles. His relation to the business community is such that he is forced in many instances—not in every instance...he has some choices. But he is forced in many instances to succumb and to be beholden to the powerful business community in Los Angeles. Why? Because they will leave; unemployment will increase; Los Angeles will become unattractive to business—big business at work...which means what?...which means big business reshaping the space in the city so you get renaissance: buildings in the cities and the homeless increases. You get shopping malls on the outside—public assembly, but private property...malls on the outside with tremendous funds, but school systems collapsing, public health collapsing, bridges collapsing and other infrastructures collapsing. I won't even talk about public transportation in Los Angeles, because L.A. lives in the Middle Ages when it comes to public transportation—a big city like this and people can't move around other than just cars and buses. What's going on? How are these people gonna get around if a car is the only way you can do it? Something is wrong...private interests of the car industry. They don't care how crowded the highways are. They want you to buy the cars—it's money—it's big business. And the only reason New York and Philadelphia have subways is because they were able to do it much earlier when they had reform administrations in the City Council and the municipal government, because they could never pull it off after the 1950s. That's why L.A. never had a chance—economic interest—too strong.

What does this have to do with black politics? Well, it makes it very difficult. Why?...because as you and I know very clearly...American politics (be they black politics, white or what-have-you) are principally a televisual and managerial politics. It is all about images. It is all about how you are packaged. It is all about how you are presented based on your sales manager who is called your adviser. There's not too much debate going on in politics. There's not too much critical exchange going on in politics these days. It is much more of images, packaging and so forth, which means then that there is what?...A decline in popular mobilization. Politicians don't mobilize people. What they do is they energize you for a moment for television and then, poof, they are gone. This is true even of the great Jesse Jackson. It's true for Jesse Jackson. If he didn't have the churches, he would have very little organization because what he has the ability to do—given his tremendous charisma and eloquence—is bring folk together quickly, and then after the speech...pick up. To be able to create an organization that will stay together and work day by day and week by week—it's hard to do. His organization—a mile wide but an inch deep. Why it's just not Jesse's fault. He's living in the televisual age, and he masters it too—sometimes too much for me. Jesse is everywhere; he's everywhere. He's gonna be there when Mandela is released. If they had a crisis in Ireland, he's gonna be in Ireland. And you know he's not taking his organization. He's taking a few employees, and he's there for TV. I'm not saying this to put Jesse down. He's responding to circumstances, you see. King had an organization. SCLC was rooted in the community. Malcolm X had an organization. Fannie Lou Hamer, National Welfare Rights Organization—she had an organization. She was rooted. It wasn't a dazzling performance, you see. It is a very different quality of leadership—a very different quality of leadership. So when we look then at politics, we have to ask what form will progressive and black politics take. I'm going to leave the question for the moment and return later.

I'm going to say something about culture and then come back and give some sense of what strategies and tactics ought to be. But I want to say something about culture, because I think culture is most important. Why is culture most important?...precisely because big business has now moved into culture. It's a culture industry. Advertising is the major force behind American culture. It is a culture of consumption that promotes an addiction to stimulation so that those stimulated consume. Consumerism and compulsive spending is at the center of the culture. It creates one of the most vicious constructs known to humankind. It is called a market morality and market mentality. And it has thoroughly penetrated the black community to such a degree that the buying and selling of commodities are such that human life means little. It is nothing but a market mentality and a market morality, and it mirrors the larger market morality and mentality of this society. That's why crack is the contemporary expression of our culture. It's ugly; it's nasty. Crack is the highest known form of addiction to stimulation that the human brain can take. It will provide levels of pleasure ten times more than orgiastic pleasure. And this culture is about pleasure. It is about orgiastic pleasure. It is about stimulation and it's about consumerism, and crack brings all of those together. That's why it's a major form of escapism in our culture—and especially in the black community. That's what's tragic about it. It's a logical expression of it. And our young brothers and sisters who are engaged in this entrepreneurial activity of buying and selling are mirroring Wall Street. They can teach at Harvard Business School, with their ingenious strategies for selling. This cultural consumption, this hedonism and consumerism, this narcissism and privatism, concerned only about one's own private project, has thoroughly shaped our young people because they are products of televisual culture. And what it has produced is the decomposition of black civil society—the shattered families and the shattered neighborhoods, you see.

The church is struggling against the influence of mass media. Many churches—sometimes most churches—succumbing to mass media, so that the sermons become melodramatic commercials for Jesus, and the prayers become "let's make a deal with God." It is nothing but a reflection of culture. You do something for me, I'll do something for me. Let's move. No, thy will be done—no, no; that's old time religion. You do something for me, I'll do something for you, is the consumer religion of our day. What do you want done?...a car, a girlfriend, new clothes—and that becomes the measure of God's blessings. This is penetrating the church itself. It's market morality, market mentality, permeating, colonizing the culture. Conversion suddenly overnight—crocodile tears. You know, Jimmy Swaggart crying every week. I learned in Sunday School that conversion was a lifelong process of struggle—ups and downs, valleys and mountain tops and so forth—not an overnight affair. That's part of the problem...too many hot Christians that get cold quick—come in fired up—three years later they moving out. There's not enough 40-year-old Christians, 40-year struggling Christians. I don't want to just focus on the Christian issue here, because I don't want to be parochial or provincial. We have many non-Christian brothers and sisters both here and in our community, but I do believe that the black churches will play a fundamental role, so I'm just highlighting the degree to which market mentality and market morality has actually moved towards the major institution in black civil society which is the black church.

Now where do we go from here? I don't want to just lay out a laundry list. But I'm trying to give us some sense of why this is a critical moment. And let's be honest. It's gonna be very difficult because the country itself is finding itself in such deep crisis. It is rendering our situation more and more visible only in its most negative forms—criminality, negative stereotypes and massive media, you see. What are we to do? Well, first economically, there are two things that we have to do. One is we have to recognize that we still need a strong black business class, which means we still need to expand black entrepreneurial activity legally. I'm not talking about illegal black entrepreneurial activity, but legal forms. But we also have to recognize that the black business class in no way has or will have in the near future the capacity to enhance the situation of most black people. This is where I violently disagree with Minister Farrakhan. I disagree with Farrakhan on a host of other things, but his economic program also needs examination. Farrakhan argues that black business expansion is the means for black enhancement and black liberation, and I say no. Why?...because you need to understand the internal dynamics of the economy. It is a corporate-dominated economy and black business is locked into the entrepreneurial sector of the economy, and the entrepreneurial sector of the economy plays a noteworthy role, but not as crucial a role as big business.

Look at the Fortune 500, and no black business is there. I hope Mr. Johnson and a host of other black businessmen continue to stretch out because they can serve as an infrastructure for black activity—both political and cultural, but there will be tremendous limits so that the expansion of the black business class, which is to say within the entrepreneurial sector of small business, must be conjoined with a critical support of the labor movement. This is very important, because the labor movement is the major movement in American progressive politics that does have assets to revenues, money. Now, some people call labor big labor as if it's the same as big business. No, this is not true. Only 18 percent of American workers are unionized. 18 percent— it's the lowest of any of the modern nations in the world. Australia is 75 percent. Sweden is 85 percent. Britain is 65 percent. The United States is 18 percent. Why?...because large numbers of American workers work for big business, and big business does not encourage unionization. But the labor movement is very important, and what is so fascinating about it is that many of the dynamic black leaders in the next ten years are going to emerge out of that labor movement. You had Bill Lucy last year. He is one example, but there's a large number of black women as well. We have got to keep track of that labor movement owing to both its attempt to bring a critique to bear on the maldistribution of wealth and its struggle for the expansion of wages and benefits for ordinary working people.

Politically, what should be the strategy and tactic? Here, we should proceed on an inside/outside strategy. We must have progressive politicians on the inside creating space for possibilities to take the form of redistribution of resources. There is nothing wrong with black mayors. Black mayors are not Pharaohs the way the older mayors have been. But none of them are Moses...none of them...they are managers, and they look out for black interests—usually black middle-class interests—rarely black under-class or working poor interests, but it's still some black interest, better than the old Pharaohs. We understand black politicians' limitations. We support them critically, and when it's time to push them out, we've got to push them out. I recall when Andy Young tried to crush the strike of the sanitation workers in Atlanta in 1976, and, of course, the image of Andy Young crushing a sanitation workers' strike and King's death in Memphis while struggling for sanitation workers is quite striking. And we asked Andy as a friend—as a brother—in fact he's a frat brother of my father...we said, Andy, what are you doing, brother?...cause I want to understand somebody's situation before I criticize them. I want to understand what limitations and constraints have been imposed on them before I just engage in my critique. That's important. So I wanted to get a sense: why are you doing this? What are your options? What alternatives are available to you? And Andy made it clear. He said, I'm struggling with a business community that's trying to string me up, and that Atlanta business community can string some folk up—not literally, but symbolically, and rhetorically and politically—which means your political life is over. And he said, you know I want to in many ways side with them, but they are pushing too far. If they didn't push so far, I would support them, but they are pushing too far. Of course, that's the very language that was used against the Civil Rights Movement. They are pushing too far. How can they be pushing too far when they are trying to survive—trying to feed their kids? What do you mean, too far? The business community is pushing too far, brother. That's the problem. I understood his options, but then I launched my critique. But when I launched it, Andy understood that it had some semblance of integrity, because I did try to understand what he was up against. And he understood the moral grounds of my critique.

Inside/outside strategy—there must be folk on the inside in politics, institutions right across the board. But, of course, I stand before you as someone who is very much on the inside of an elite institution, Princeton University. I'm very much on the inside. Toni Morrison and Nell Painter and others—we work on the inside of that institution with its racist and patriarchal heritage to create more space for students and present them with alternative views—black, white, red—right across the board. It's an uphill struggle, but there must be those on the outside, and this has been the downfall in the last ten years. This is why Farrakhan emerges. This is why Al Sharpton emerges. This is why

Kwame Toure can go across campuses around this country presenting his revolutionary socialism that has lost touch with black America. And I just, in fact, talked with Kwame at Princeton. Just on Wednesday, I moderated a session that Mark and I were talking about. Now, I admire and respect Kwame very deeply because he was one of the great courageous freedom fighters in the 1960s. There is no doubt about it. He is willing to give his life every day, and he has been in and out of Africa for eighteen years. But the point is that Kwame Toure, Minister Louis Farrakhan, the early Al Sharpton and a whole host of garden-variety prophets are trying to fill the vacuum left by elected public officials who themselves cannot speak with boldness and defiance of the white power structure and young people are more and more open to this kind of language. They want to hear a critique, and so they are looking for somebody and looking for someone.

You heard just the other day that Columbia University students invited Professor Griff, a young rapper, to speak on education in the year 2000. Professor Griff is a highly talented artist who is the DJ of Public Enemy, which is one of the leading rap groups in America—one of the leaders of the hip-hop nation. Professor Griff has said some rather vicious things about Jewish brothers and sisters. He says, for example, that most of the wickedness on the globe is due to Jews. He says the reason why Jew is in jewelry is because Jews themselves concocted the term and the industry, and it has been regulated for the last 400 years, and on and on and on. I mean, it's vicious. It's wrong; it's immoral; it's false; it's off the wall, but this is the kind of rhetoric you get out of a brother 19 years old trying to make sense of the world. Now whether he needs to be sitting up at Columbia University talking about education in the year 2000 is a different issue. All you educators out there, think about it. But you know, the first thing I thought of when I read that, I said to myself, "we black intellectuals and educators must be really failing our young people." What a critique of me—not that they should invite me, but I think of all of the dynamic and insightful and visionary black educators across the country, and they choose Professor Griff. But they don't know about these black educators. They don't know about black intellectuals. They are too busy pursuing their careers. They are too busy engaging their research with no links whatsoever to these young people, whereas Professor Griff is out there cutting those records and the young people are buying those records, and the talented Chuck D is writing those lyrics. A lot of the lyrics make a lot of sense. Some of them are off the wall, but a lot of them make a lot of sense. And the young people are more shaped by mass media than they are by those older institutions I was talking about—family, neighborhood, church, fraternities, sororities and so forth. They go for Professor Griff.

There is a vacuum in black leadership. Think about it preachers. Think about it deacons. Think about it sisters. Preachers don't have a monopoly on leadership. Leadership is earned. It's not through birthright that you gain it. Black preachers have been leaders because they earned it, but they don't always earn it. Laity...be aware. You can be leaders, too, if you earn it. Gather your courage. There's a vacuum out there. And to the degree to which we do not have the prophetic voices from the outside working with the progressive voices from the inside, the crisis in black leadership will continue. We have progressive leadership on the inside—Maxine Waters, Ronald Dellums, Major Owens. What's the serious brother who pastors the church in Philadelphia? Yes, Bill Gray. These are serious leaders. But all of that energy is on the inside, you see, and little on the outside. Jesse is fascinating because he has moved from prophet to politician. He can't really decide which one he really wants to be. Because if you are on the inside, it's a world of compromise. We all know that in our jobs. It's a world of compromise. You have to know how to work it, you see. You have to get mad at the right time, not the wrong time. You don't want all your energy on that battle when there's a bigger one coming on. But we need leaders on the outside. We don't have it, and until we get it we are going to get Farrakhan presenting his black business strategy; we are going to get Farrakhan preoccupied with Jewish folk, losing sight of their humanity oftentimes; we are gonna get the early Sharpton—though courageous—running around thinking that somehow he gets wisdom by osmosis rather than reading and studying. It's crude leadership. Yet, in a sense, I have a respect for Sharpton because he tries to do all he can with what he has. That's admirable—despite my disagreements with him. Think of what those to whom much is given will do if they did all that they could with what they had. This is a very important point, a very important point.

But moving on to culture. What do we do? We have on the one hand supporters at the economic level of black business. I like that new magazine, *Emerge*. Have you seen *Emerge*? Has anybody seen *Emerge*? Yes...take a look at it. There's enough room in black America for *Ebony* and *Emerge*. It's a serious magazine. It's got enough glitz to survive. It's still part of the televisual culture—image-centered culture, but it's got some politics that raises deep questions for young folk, you see. The black business class stretching out. Stay strong Wilber Ames, Jr.! The young folk are stretching out.

Also in the recording industry...I like MC Hammer, not because he can move so quick. I know a lot of brothers and sisters who can move on the street. But MC Hammer is a business man. And I think he knows how to use his money, you see. People look at Prince. What's wrong with that man, showing up in his jock strap? He must have lost *his* mind. Oh no, no, no, no, no. Prince is not only a great artist, listen to the Lord's Prayer on one of his albums. Prince is a business man. Every year he gives thousands of dollars to the United Negro College Fund—thousands of dollars to black colleges. But he doesn't say a word about it. He was just in Minneapolis giving that money out. He's a business man. There are very few people who get access to him and talk to him about what he should do with some of this money.

The same is true of our athletes. When they are wise, they are investing in the black community in order to enhance, and many do. Magic Johnson and others do. That is part of the black business class too, to create some more infrastructures, but it is not the cure for our ills. That's why the labor movement is crucial.

Inside/outside strategy for politics. What do we do with culture? Here we come to religion. Here we come to religion. As well as cultural workers in mass media, journalists, TV consultants, who are all trying to hold back the market mentality and market morality in the country in general and in black America in particular. It is a difficult struggle. It is a struggle which must be waged in the name of non-market values. For those of us who are Christians, love becomes the crucial value. It is a non-market value. It mitigates against market mentality. It mitigates against market morality. But love is not the only one. There is loyalty. That's a term nobody uses anymore. Why? Because we live in a culture of betrayal on the personal level, on the collective level, on the societal level. Think of what must have been going through Marion Barry's mind when he looked up at Mrs. Moore when the FBI hit him...betrayal, sheer betrayal. Now, he's wrong as two left shoes, but it is still the act of betrayal that gets him. Think about it. Who can you trust? Who is committed enough that you own a common project together so you won't be betrayed in the long run? Think of the debate right now around the text about Ralph Abernathy. I just raised a question. I'm not going into that debate. We can go on and on. Loyalty is a non-market value.

Last is freedom. Freedom is actually a non-market value. Now see, we are going to have a tremendous problem with this because of the recent exciting developments in Eastern Europe with the collapse of that ugly Stalinist form of regimentation and repression of the population in Eastern Europe. But the response of America is what?...freedom means the market. You see how you define freedom in market terms rather than non-market terms? No, freedom doesn't mean the market. Market is one of the means by which freedom may be achieved when there are jobs, health- and child-care, education and so forth. But it is an attempt to flatten out the notion of freedom into a market conception. And this is what we are getting at. What they really want is a market? No, they want freedom, and some of them think that the market will give them freedom. They need to consult us so we can let them know some of the more vicious effects of the market. We remember the slave option. That was the market. But we also believe that the market is one of the means if it is regulated in such a way that human need is at the center, so that non-market values of love and loyalty and freedom must be promoted and encouraged on every level, and I am still old enough to think that the prophetic juices that flow in black America will still come primarily, but not exclusively, from the prophetic wing of the black church. And I say that not as the Christian who has my own biases, but I also say it as one who tries to understand the history of black folk and where large numbers of black people are who have access to non-market values like love and loyalty and freedom, that have the courage enough to bring critique to bear on a society that is deeply conservative and obsessed with business.

You have to be able to generate certain kinds of character, you see. We have had motivational structures collapse in our society. When we have enough character and integrity to lead this kind of movement, more than likely it will come out of those kinds of institutions such as the black church. This is what I will have to say to you this morning, and I look forward to dialogue, questions, queries, responses, comments or what-have-you.

Thank you so very much for allowing me to go on so long.

Prophetic Theology

"...our theology must name the sins and evils that surround us and the salvation that we are hoping for..."

Kairos Document, 4.1

The Kairos Document is a call to action and for solidarity from oppressed Christians in the belly of one beast to us Christians in the belly of another beast. And the link between those beasts has to be part of our investigation. Prophetic Theology cuts much deeper than the intellect; Prophetic Theology forces us to exemplify in our own lives what we espouse in our rhetoric. It raises questions of integrity, questions of character, and, most importantly, questions of risk and sacrifice. One of the things that inspires me about the South African theologians and Christians is that they are caught in a whirlwind, so that, like in the early church, to be a Christian means to risk and to sacrifice.

In South Africa it is a crime to hope; to be a serious Christian is to commit a crime, just as for the early Christians to be a Christian meant to end up in the lion's den. And this is in many ways alien to us First World Christians. In our postmodern culture, a culture of depthlessness, of surfaces, of commodities, commitment itself becomes a commodity. Commitment itself becomes fashionable. Some even make careers on it. One of the things I learned in my visit to South Africa in the summer of 1985 was that to be a Christian, in a serious sense, means that you have to come to terms with death.

So Prophetic Theology goes far, far beyond the kind of disciplinary division of labor that we see within our academic institutions. We're talking about living a certain kind of life. Some of our grandmothers understand this. We young folk, in many instances, have to be called back, and ironically called back by young heroes in South Africa who are willing to give their lives, to sacrifice, and to do it daily.

We find three basic components in Prophetic Theology. The first is a religious conception of what it is to be human, of how we are to act, of what we are to hope for. We'll put this under the rubric of *religious vision*.

The second crucial component is *historical and social analysis*, which is simply a set of tools or intellectual analytical weapons that help us in a struggle. The context is a battlefield, struggle, resistance, contestation.

The third component is *action*, what will we do? Lord, what will you have us to do? We must name our action, praxis, strategies, tactics.

Religious Vision

We begin with *imago dei*, being made in the image of God. Can we take seriously the radical egalitarian implication of the notion that God made all human beings in God's image and that therefore all individuals are unique and distinctive and have a sanctity and dignity of their own, that they therefore have equal status and warrant a particular type of treatment? The doctrine of *imago dei* is, on the one hand, radically egalitarian. On the other hand it is radically universalistic, but is targeted on those who are denied dignity and a certain minimum of humane treatment.

The very notion of humane treatment is inseparable from historical struggle. Humane treatment four hundred years ago was very different from what it is now. But it means a Christian mandate for identification with the downtrodden, the dispossessed, the disinherited, with the exploited and the oppressed. The doctrine of *imago dei* also accents individuals, individuals in community. It means that individuals are never reducible to community. It holds at arm's length any authoritarian communitarianism and it promotes a healthy communitarianism. Individuals are unintelligible without the community, but the individual is irreducible to the community as well. We all die by ourselves. We all struggle with despair and dread, each in our own way. In this complex dialectical interplay between individual and community we must not lose sight of our religious vision.

A second dimension of our religious vision is fallenness, the doctrine of sin. We are finite and fallen and therefore there ought to be institutional mechanisms that insure that fallen human beings not abuse their power. Lord Acton is right: absolute power corrupts absolutely. Radical democracy is the best we finite, fallen creatures can do. Democracy is an ethical implication of the Christian conception of what it is to be human. The question is how we understand democracy. What is its content? What is its substance?

The third dimension of our religious vision has to do with the coming of the kingdom, with the empowerment that flows from the inbreaking and invading of a kingdom that on the one hand is beyond our power and on the other is inseparable from what we can do. We are kingdom-bound. We are never kingdom-creating, but we stay in contact with its power. People tend to think that religious talk is different from political talk. You can talk about a kingdom, but it's just a metaphor, just an image. No, it's very real. You have to have deep, deep religious faith to stay in the struggle for a long time. Ask anybody who's been in the struggle for a long time. You have to have deep faith. For Christians it means digging deep into the depths of what kingdom-talk is about. That's our primary source of empowerment.

If you haven't dealt with the bondage of death and despair, then you're going to be disillusioned, just like some secular leftists who struggle for five years and then go live the good life. They haven't dug deep enough. This is not a sprint; this is a marathon. The Kairos Document understands that. So when we talk about kingdom, we talk about empowerment. We talk about something that fundamentally impinges upon those who are attempting to be serious

Christians. I like the talk about hope in the Kairos Document. We live in a time when hope itself has been called into question as a category. That's why the cynicism is so pervasive. Possibility itself is called into question. That's what it means to live at the end of the age of Europe and in the middle of the Americanization and Sovietization of the world.

Anybody who takes hope seriously and possibility seriously is going to look like a fool in our world. Weber talked about the world as an iron cage. Adorno talks about the iron cage in Marxist terms. They call hope in question. Often they invoke holocaust to describe the evil in the midst of a civilized Europe. The holocaust is one of the grand evils of human history, yet it doesn't impose a closure on hope. It might for those who have a parochial vision, a Eurocentric vision, more than for those who have been dealing with many holocausts down through the corridors of time.

Historical and Social Analysis

The second component of Prophetic Theology accented by the Kairos Document is historical and social analysis. I cannot overemphasize how important this analysis is. But I'm not making a fetish of it; it is only a weapon. It is important because there is a sense in which everybody these days agrees on values. Botha and Reagan claim to be for freedom; I'm for freedom; you're for freedom. But if everybody agrees on values, why do we have these fundamental conflicts? When I debate Michael Novak and other Christian neo-conservatives, we all step up and talk about how we're for democracy, we're for liberty, we're for freedom. And then he goes on to support the U.S. invasion in Nicaragua. The difference is that in many instances we have a different historical and social analysis. We understand power differently. We understand wealth differently. We understand the circulation of influence and prestige differently. And so the battle within the Christian tradition is often a battle over which historical and social analysis we are deploying. The question is whether that analysis is informed by a Christocentric perception, informed by the cross—capital *c*—as well as the many crosses—small *c*—that people have to bear every day.

Historical and social analysis means that we have to have some sense of the larger context, the larger forces that shape and mold not only who we are but our projection of where we want to go. Again there are three points I want to mention here. The first has to do with the Europeanization of the world. The age of Europe began in 1492. It reached its peak in the nineteenth and early twentieth centuries. By Europe I mean the handful of nations between the Atlantic Ocean and the Ural mountains. In 1835 they owned 35 percent of the globe, and by 1918 they owned 87 percent of the globe. This went hand in hand with the subjugation of non-European peoples as well as the exploitation of European workers. That is the backdrop of what we're dealing with. It is inseparable from the emergence of the capitalist mode of production, social relations of production, the creation of various classes in which one class owns the land and instruments of production and the majority of human beings are forced to sell themselves like commodities, that is, sell their time, their energy, and their skills in order to stay alive. In the nineteenth century if you didn't find a job you starved. These conditions of industrial market capitalism have changed only after the tremendous, protracted struggles of oppressed people.

There is a small dose of humanity within first world capitalism. But when we look at the Third World we can see just what capitalism once looked like, because there it is still ugly and brutish and nasty and oppressive. What is distinctive in many ways about South Africa is that it still maintains the legacy and the residue of the Europeanization of the world, because it is still an old colonial regime. Europe was in decline and the United States and the Soviet Union began to emerge. But in South Africa we can still see indigenous people. The United States is not vastly different, because the United States, like Australia and Canada, is a European settler society too. U.S. experience began with the dispossession of people's land, extermination, genocide. Just go to a reservation to be reminded of American history from a point of view different from that of the mainstream. In South Africa the indigenous population was able to resist, and they were rendered useful as cheap labor. They are still there and they aren't going anywhere. They continue to resist. It is an old legacy.

By the 1970s most of Africa had begun to burst out of the older form of Europeanization, though we know it continues in neo-colonial forms. We in the United States recognize that our country, like South Africa, had to engage in an anti-colonial and anti-imperialistic struggle against Britain. That is one of the ironies of being an American. There is a sense in which the United States, the nation born modern, born liberal, born bourgeois, was once a revolutionary country, even as it subjugated people of African descent. The Declaration of Independence sounds revolutionary. They were talking not only about a change within a government, but the human power to change fundamentally the structures of government themselves. That's what the slave master Jefferson wrote about. He had revolutionary blood flowing in some parts of his veins. We won't talk about the other parts, in relation to his slaves. But there is an important revolutionary tradition in what is now one of the major counter-revolutionary powers in the world. A similar process occurred in South Africa. The Afrikaners struggled against British imperialism and then subjected the indigenous populations to subjugation.

There is no doubt in my mind that if the South had won the Civil War, there would still be apartheid in the South. In fact for the most part we had apartheid up until 1964: the crypto-fascist terrorism, the institutionalized racism, the lynching, that strange fruit that southern trees bore that Billie Holiday sang so poignantly about. It would all still be here if it were not for the penetration of capital from the North and the emergence of liberal elites within a Democratic Party that began opening itself to the movement of Martin Luther King, Jr., and others. Apartheid is not far removed from the American experience. The parallels have much to say to us.

Dealing then with historical and social analysis as tools, as weapons, we begin to look at other institutional forms that deny life. I have talked about economics, but we can also talk about the repression of the State. State repression occurs not only in South Africa. The population of our prisons is 47 percent black and brown, but blacks represent only 11 percent of the population, and our brown brothers and sisters only another 7 percent. South Africa is up against one of the most brutal apparatuses known to humankind. It is a counter-insurgency State that specializes in smashing insurgents. We could point to Chile and Korea as well. This State repression goes hand in hand with economic exploitation. Look at the response to strikes in South Africa. It looks like Rockefeller in 1877. Rockefeller had a vigilante group bigger than the state military in Ohio. The U.S. had a very weak state from 1877 to 1920. That's one of the reasons we had robber barons and tremendous consolidation of wealth among power elites.

When South Africans go on strike, the repressive apparatus comes down. But you cannot rule a society solely by force. You can attempt to, but over time you need something else. You either have to convince the people to consent to their oppression or you have to attempt to marginalize those who refuse to consent. Even the repressive State apparatus in South Africa cannot rule by sheer force; the Kairos Document is an example of that. Like the Confessing Church in Nazi Germany, the Kairos Document shows that the human spirit refuses to be completely snuffed out. Those of us who are Christian believe this has something to do with the God we worship, with the grounds of hope so foolish in the eyes of many.

My second point in relation to historical and social analysis is *racism*. Racism is inseparable from economic exploitation and State repression, but it is not identical to them. Racism has its own specificity. The white European supremacist practices that are institutionalized in the everyday life of South Africans and are still often operative in this country have their own life and logic. They are related to but are not subsumable under the economy. Racism is embodied in the child's question, Why do white folks treat black folks so bad? Some say that this is an anachronistic question: it used to be the case, but we've undergone tremendous progress. I say no, we have to keep asking the question.

Africans understand what it is to be culturally and aesthetically degraded and devalued by non-Africans. The degradation works on a personal level and has to do with identity and subjectivity, with how you conceive of yourself, with whether you have the capacity or whether you think you have the capacity to affirm your own potential. We see this every day in black children.

Third, we must mention the *subjugation of women*. Patriarchal practices, the degrading and devaluating and the marginalizing, pervade all other practices. One might raise the so-called women's question within both first world and third world contexts. But the women's question is not a strategic question, it is a Christian one. If we talk about evil, we're going to talk about subjugation. Don't shy away from evil if you're a Christian. Look at it for what it is and try to come to terms with it. And ask the Lord Christ to empower you to struggle against it.

Action

To be a Christian is fundamentally to live a certain kind of life, to live a sacrificial life, a love-informed life, a life of care and a life of giving. The question then becomes how to live a Christian life in a context in which the class and race contradictions are so intense that there is civil war. How do you live in that kind of brokenness? This is one of the questions I see emerging from the Prophetic Theology of the Kairos Document. And the crucial question then becomes, What are the alternatives? What are the options? None of us is born under circumstances of our own choosing, whether in the biological sense or in the familial sense. The scope of our options will be very different depending on our context. The United States presents a certain set of options, still very, very limited. How do you deal with a two-party system that is basically run by the economic and political elites of the country? What kind of progressive alternatives are there? Do you work on the local level and struggle with Brother Harold Washington in Chicago? Can there be more Washingtons across the country and less Bradleys? An important question. Bradley's still better than the alternative in Los Angeles. This shows you how bad things are.

The context in South Africa is even more limited and more intense because the blood flows more freely. Raise the issue of armed struggle with first world Christians and they usually tend to shake a bit, as if they didn't have a history of armed struggle, as if their ancestors didn't fight in the anti-capitalist armed guerrilla Revolutionary War of America in 1776 or in the Civil War in 1860. As if they didn't go marching off to World War I and couldn't wait to march off to World War II. Don't talk about armed struggle to oppressed people until you understand your own history.

On the other hand armed struggle is no plaything either. It reminds us of just how tragic the human condition can actually be. I have great respect for nonviolent leaders like Martin Luther King, Jr., Allan Boesak, and others. I don't agree with them, but I have great respect for them. I think that those within the Christian tradition who unequivocally refuse to accept violence advocate a respectable position, although not persuasive to me. I think those who hold this position play a role, but I don't think they are going to be major agents in the making of history. They represent a moral position that reminds us of how tragic our situation is. But given the tragedy it seems to me that there certainly are circumstances in which Christians ought to engage in armed struggle. I can certainly envision myself doing so. I believe that we should never advocate any position that we are not willing to accept ourselves.

To accept armed struggle the situation has to be extreme. All alternatives have to be exhausted and you have to be able to point to historical evidence that they are exhausted. Most importantly you have to be able to point to the probable success of armed struggle. It cannot be simply adolescent rebellion. It has to be worked out, with detailed and elaborate strategies and tactics. George Washington understood this. There might be a point, in various parts of the globe including South Africa, where Christians will be forced to engage in armed struggle. Far be it from me to pontificate on this from Chicago; I'm simply raising the possibility.

There are other forms of struggle as well. The role of the church is in the community organizations. One thinks of course of the United Democratic Front and other such groups. The role of the church can vary. In the United States the church has a crucial role in various local progressive organizations. These days such organizations are not very popular, but they can continue to hold the line so that maybe by the 1990s, when things begin to be shaken up again, these organizations can emerge just as they did in the 1950s.

The last point of political strategy is the role of labor. I think in South Africa this is especially important because of the central role of industrial workers and the contribution that their organization can make to community action groups. In the United States the issue of labor is different, but still very important. As we undergo deindustrialization, the high-tech revolution, the new collar and white collar and brown collar revolutions, labor takes on a very different configuration. It becomes much more heterogeneous, much more diverse. This means that there will be different ways and different patterns in which organizing moves. Blacks, browns, and women will more and more become the cutting edge of the labor movement, linked in interracial solidarity. Where are our churches in relation to our progressive trade unions? That's one thing we can learn from both South Africa and the Kairos Document. We must refuse to give up the best of those long traditions of struggle, often times in flawed ways, for democracy, for justice.

I hope that the Kairos Document inspires the first world, North America, that it infuses us with the depth of commitment that is displayed by the pen put to paper of that document. There is a sense in which American culture is becoming more and more a kind of wasteland, a wasted possibility, an unrealized potentiality. We are in deep need of inspiration. We are in deep need of seeing human beings, and especially Christians, in social motion. There will be no change in America, there will be no change in South Africa, there will be no change in Chile or Nicaragua, until there are human beings in social motion. The possibility of social motion is kept alive by the grand gift that has been given to us. The gift of the Kairos Document is another form of God's empowerment for us to continue to struggle.

On Black Rage

American culture seems to lack two elements basic to
race relations: a deep sense of the tragic and a genuine grasp
of the unadulterated rage directed at American society. The
chronic refusal of most Americans to understand the sheer
absurdity that confronts a person of African descent in this
country—the incessant assaults on black intelligence,
beauty, character and possibility—is not simply a matter of
defending white-skin privilege. It also bespeaks a reluctance to look squarely at the brutal side and tragic dimension of the American past and present. Such a long and hard
look would puncture the life-sustaining bubble of many
Americans, namely that this nation of undeniable opportunities and freedom-loving people committed unspeakable
crimes against other human beings, especially black people.

Unfortunately, this fact has become trivialized—
partly by black middle-class opportunists—into a cynical
move in a career game of upmanship that reinforces white
guilt and paralysis. Yet, as our great artists like Ralph Elli-
son, William Faulkner, Lillian Smith and Toni Morrison
have shown, the tragic plight and brutal treatment of black
people is a constitutive element—not a mere moral mis-
take—of American civilization. To put it crudely, America
would not exist without 244 years of black slavery, 87 years
of Jim and Jane Crow (including the lynching of a black
man, woman or child every three days for a quarter of a
century) and now one of two black kids caught in a vio-
lence-infested life of poverty.

Black responses to this unique American experience
have been shot through with rage, just as were Jewish responses to attacks, assaults, and pogroms in anti-Semitic
Russia and Eastern Europe at the turn of the century. Yet
xenophobic czars and authorities were not surprised at Jewish rage. Would not any vicious tyrants expect this response

from their victims? In stark contrast, most American elites, owing to narrow self-serving notions of freedom and justice, have been flabbergasted at the expression of black rage. This is so even though most black rage has not been directed at American elites, but rather at other black people (especially women), Italian shopkeepers, gays and lesbians, and Jewish entrepreneurs. These targeted expressions of black rage, though often downright cowardly and petty, signify the social invisibility and relative powerlessness of a people toward whom American elites have been and are indifferent.

The 60s is a watershed period because black rage came out of the closet. As white institutional terrorism was challenged, black rage surfaced with a power and potency never seen in American history. In fact, it threatened the very social order and stability of the country. The major American elite response to this threat was to reduce tragic black persons into pathetic black victims and to redirect the channels of black rage in and to black working class and poor communities. The reduction was done by making black poor people clients of a welfare system that both sustained and degraded them; by viewing black middle-class people as questionable and stigmatized beneficiaries of affirmative action programs that fuelled their identity crises; and by rendering black working people (the majority of black people!) as nearly nonexistent even as their standard and quality of living significantly declined.

The high social costs borne by much of black America during the Republican years of recession and "recovery" have been devastating. Measured in terms of housing, education, jobs, health care and, above all, the massive social and moral breakdown in nurturing black youth, we may be at a point of no return. And yet the chickens now coming home to roost are not the ones we expected. Instead of a focus on the fundamental sources of black social misery—the maldistribution of wealth and power filtered through our corporate, financial and political elites, we find black rage directed at racist ethnic individuals and communities, mere small players in the larger game of power in the city, state and country.

Some of the blame can be put at the feet of black leadership. In New York City, Mayor David Dinkins, a decent man in a desperate situation, has failed to make the requisite symbolic gestures to the black community in his efforts to disarm white charges of personal bias and racial favoritism. This strategy has backfired. Community spokespersons, like Rev. Al Sharpton and Rev. Herbert Daughtry, two steadfast and courageous activists locked into an endless cycle of immediate reactions to events, are, at times and out of frustration, swept into a rhetoric that embraces the lowest common denominator of black rage. The slide from demands of justice and due process to those of vengeance and vigilantism is a short one for an abused and enraged people. Yet, as Revs. Sharpton and Daughtry at their best recognize, this slide is neither morally right nor politically effective.

Elijah Muhammed and Martin Luther King, Jr. understood one fundamental truth about black rage: it must be neither ignored nor ignited. This is what separates them from the great Malcolm X. Malcolm indeed articulated black rage in a manner unprecedented in American history; yet his broad black nationalist platforms were too vague to give this black rage any concrete direction. Elijah and Martin knew how to work with black rage in a constructive manner: shape it through moral discipline, channel it into political organization and guide it by visionary leadership. Black rage is as American as apple pie. This is why the future of our city, state and country depend, in large part, on whether we acknowledge it, how we respond to it, and the manner in which bold and wise leaders direct it.

We Socialists

Reflections about the future of the Left after Communism force us, it seems to me, to raise three fundamental questions. The first is: Where are we? The second is: What is to be done? And the third is: How to do it?

There are moments in human history in which there are bitter ironic turns and brutal triumphs of hypocrisy. That defines our moment. In Eastern Europe, the negation of so-called Communist regimes breeds a distrust of the very idea of socialism, alongside a fetishizing of the market as some panacea for the undeniable human suffering perpetrated by repressive and regimenting regimes. The triumph of hypocrisy is what we have seen in the Middle East, in which the first major war after the so-called Cold War results in a reconstitution of *Pax Americana*.

It cannot but leave us personally depressed, intellectually demoralized and politically discouraged. And all of us are struggling with this, and we have to hit it head-on. We have to be honest about it.

The question becomes, then, what ought our response be, in the belly of the major empire in the world—as the other empire tragically disintegrates and collapses—and coming out of a grand, but weak and feeble, left tradition in this country, in which the sacred cow is economic growth by means of corporate priorities; founded on the dead bodies and dispossessed land of indigenous peoples, and scarred bodies of African slaves, and marginalized hands and feet of the poor peasants from Europe who made their way here in the latter part of the 19th century, and the domesticating of women.

Our Identity Crisis

How do we think seriously *as a Left*, given this fright-

239

ening and terrifying moment? It sees to me, in response to the first question, that we have an identity crisis; we have an intellectual crisis; we have an organizational crisis.

What does it mean to be a socialist at this moment? What is the relation between socialist identity and the host of other identity politics now flooding the streets and the academy? It seems to me that to be a socialist means, if anything, to keep track of the wasted energies, the spiritual sterility, the exhausted potential left by the rule of capital—that set of interlocking elites, the banks, corporations, the political elites. If we as socialists cannot highlight the trail left by the rule of capital across national boundaries, across racial boundaries, across gender boundaries, then there is no future for the socialist Left in the U.S., and it will dissolve and degenerate into a micropolitics of single issues and identity politics.

It's a serious challenge. Why? Because if all we have are identity politics and micropolitics, then capital, now with hardly any barriers, will rule supreme, leaving more dead bodies, and more wasted energies, and more spiritual sterility.

It's a challenge. But we also recognize that more than likely, our socialist identities, our socialist politics, will be a socialist leaven in a progressive loaf, because more than likely we're not going to be the vanguard for the next wave of social motion and social movement it will be those local activists who stumble in a variety of different issues, hungry for a movement of integrity and decency and dignity. They will be open to gullibility and manipulability, yes, but hungry for a movement.

That heterogeneous mass that emerged in the 1890s and the 1930s and the 1960s will more than likely emerge again. And some of us will be brought kicking and screaming into that movement, because there will be people we don't like in terms of their culture and their beliefs and their orientations. But they'll be ready for struggle. And the challenge is, can we as socialists play a fundamental role, to make the connections and links between this heterogeneous set of activists who are willing to give their time and their lives—to push it in a left and progressive direction?

We're not strong enough to constitute the movement in and of ourselves, not in the near future. This is why our identity crisis must be confronted candidly. And we must preserve our socialist identity as we reflect on whatever other identities we may have—national identity, ethnic identity, gender identity, sexual orientation identity, racial identity and so forth.

Thinking Historically

The second level is intellectual crisis. How do we preserve a subtle historical sense, an ability to think historically and to understand the present as history?

The academic Left has taken a textualist turn, for the most part, in which history becomes dissolved into dazzling textual enactments that portray irony at its highest and become a badge of intellectual sophistication.

How do we preserve serious study of history? By this I mean actual human agents who are exerting their sense of where and what they can do under structural and institutional circumstances not of their own choosing. And this is a serious challenge as well, it's a crucial intellectual challenge.

If we lose the intellectual battle, it's going to be difficult to preserve any substantive socialist identity, let alone organizations and infrastructure. This is why this Socialist Scholars conference is so very important. Because struggles in the life of the mind are crucial political struggles, and the intellectual terrain is a crucial terrain for contestation and struggle, linked to unleashing new possibilities of vision and analysis and exemplary praxis. Thank God for the Socialist Scholars conference.

Let us go back into those terrains and contest our textual leftists, and try to bring the best of historical sociology, of Marx, of Weber, of Lukács, of Simmel, of Du Bois, of Simone de Beauvoir and others who tried to think historically.

But at the same time we must adopt a very different method than we have used in the past. Given these turns of ironies and triumphs of hypocrisy, I would think that all of us have been taught an intellectual and political humility, learning that dogmatism blinds, that orthodoxy and sectarian perspectives disenable, render us impotent.

And again the metaphor of jazz comes to me. We've got to become very much like the jazz women and jazz men, in which we're fluid and flexible and protean and open to a variety of different sources and perspectives. Ones that we thought might not have provided any source of insight might in fact be useful, as we both constitute a usable past, and project a future.

Organizationally, we're still weak on the level of infrastructure; we still have journals rather than massive organizations. And it's very important, then, to sustain local activists, be it intellectually—*The Nation, Z Magazine,* and other publications in the intellectual sphere—or be it at the neighborhood level.

Local activists must become more and more at the center of how we think about the condition for the possibility of social motion and social movement. And critiques of leaders in the limelight must be relentless, because moments of weakness generate highlighting of leaders who are unconnected, or less and less connected, to those anonymous, invisible local activists who carry the ball courageously and heroically between moments of social motion.

The Narrative about Noah

As to what is to be done: the narrative about Noah was about preserving the best of something, no matter what the circumstances were. And that's what, in part, we're about: preserving the best of our intellectual tradition. The Marx-bashing that goes on these days, in journalism, in the academy, is thoroughly anti-intellectual. Marx had no panacea, but we have a duty to preserve the best of that tradition, as we practice openness to the anti-racist, the anti-homophobic and the rich feminist intellectual tradition that has emerged in the last 25 years or so, based on earlier texts.

And so it is organizationally. One of the main reasons why I remain a member of Democratic Socialists of America—because people love to criticize me being a member of DSA, and I'm not making an advertisement pitch—I've got to be organized with some group. So in part it's out of default, you see. Because we need the groups highlighting connection and linkage in a time of balkanization and polarization and fragmentation. There's got to be some group that does this. I mean, DSA's not the only one—I have some deeper reasons for being a member, but I'm not going into that at the moment. But this is very important.

Finally, how do we do it? Here I want to suggest that after the sophisticated analysis, and after the tremendous energy invested in organization, that in the end we do it as a leap of faith and a labor of love.

There's a leap of faith in the mental and moral capacities of ordinary people. I call it democratic faith. John Dewey called it a democratic faith. Walt Whitman understood it. The early Du Bois understood it. We democratic socialists have to really believe that ordinary people are not just objects of manipulation, that they do have the potential to regulate their lives and participate at the highest levels of the decision-making process in those institutions that guide and regulate their lives. If you don't believe it, you'll lose faith in the capacity of the "masses" to really uplift themselves without educated elites, or technological toys, or nostalgia for a golden age, or claims of inevitability about progress, and so forth. All of these have been foundations to sustain a refusal to look democratic faith in the face.

Democratic faith is not a romanticizing and idealizing of ordinary persons. It's a recognition of their potential and possibility. And the labor of love has to do with the level of sacrifice needed. We're talking in part about a way of life as much as a struggle; and this is one thing I actually admire deeply in the old Communist comrades. I might have deep intellectual, ideological and moral reservations and disagreements with the old Communist comrades, but what they understood is something that a lot of black church activists understood: that if you are serious about this struggle, there's going to be levels of sacrifice that are unimaginable, but you go ahead anyway. And the only thing I can call it is a labor of love. Any other metaphor that you know that's better, fine—I accept it. But that's what it is, because that's what we're up against. So overwhelming.

And if there's any hope that we have, it's going to be precisely the degree to which we can muster the imagination, the intelligence, the joy, the laughter, to respond to the identity crisis, the intellectual crisis and the organizational crisis, based on new possibilities possibly unleashed...but maybe not. That's where we are presently, and we hope that we will be able to move forward in such a way that in the coming years we will be a little farther removed from this present moment of apparent paralysis.

About Common Courage Press

Books for an Informed Democracy

In this volume, Cornel West asks

What does it mean to be a socialist at this moment? What is the relation between socialist identity and the host of other identity politics now flooding the streets and the academy? It seems to me that to be a socialist means, if anything, to keep track of the wasted energies, the spiritual sterility, the exhausted potential left by the rule of capital—that set of interlocking elites, the banks, corporations, the political elites. If we as socialists cannot highlight the trail left by the rule of capital across national boundaries, across racial boundaries, across gender boundaries, then there is no future for the socialist Left in the U.S., and it will dissolve and degenerate into a micropolitics of single issues and identity politics.

In an effort to grapple with these issues, Common Courage Press was founded in 1991 and publishes books for social justice on race, gender, feminism, economics, ecology, indigenous issues, labor, and U.S. domestic and foreign policy. The Press seeks to provide analysis of problems from a range of perspectives and to aid activists and others in developing strategies for action.

You can reach us at:

Common Courage Press
P.O. Box 702
Monroe, ME 04951
207-525-0900 fax: 207-525-3068

Send for a free catalog!